1515 Capital of Texas Hwy.
Suite 205
Austin, Texas 78746
(512) 329-8373
(512) 329-6051 Fax
www.bardpress.com

Dear Reader,

Not long ago, under rather odd circumstances, I discovered this remarkable collection of short essays. Although written by Roy Hollister Williams as letters to his clients and friends, they contain timeless truths that reach beyond advertising and good business. They reveal the simple, profound principles that work in life, and they embody the ideals that have made America great.

As I finished my first reading, I knew I had to bring this book to a much larger audience. Each time I read the manuscript, I'm more convinced we can all find value in the Wizard's writings. *The Wizard of Ads* is certainly about advertising, marketing, friendship, and life. But I think you will discover that, at its core, it is really a book about you.

So, here, in much of its original form and spirit, is *The Wizard of Ads*. It is my pleasure to share it with you.

Ray Bard
Publisher

To the clients and friends of Roy H. Williams

Dear Friend,

Lately I've noticed that you and I are both so busy attending
to the merely urgent that we have no time for the truly important.
And it's not just you and me, it's all of America. The whole
country seems to be plunging headlong into the future without so
much as a road map sketched on the back of a napkin.

Although I know that we need to consider the future, I also
know that those who do not learn from history are destined to
repeat it. My ongoing study of advertising has led me to believe
that while technology is changing exponentially, the hearts of the
people aren't changing at all. We're still the same predictable
creatures we've always been.

People and advertising seem subject to certain laws of the
universe that are impervious to change. I believe that a knowledge
of these laws is the secret to finding yourself in the right
place, at the right time, doing the right thing in the right way.

Let's you and I make a deal. If you will agree to pause for
just six minutes a week to think about your business and your
future, I'll write you a weekly memo about the timeless truths on
which I have come to depend. At the end of a year, you will have
spent more than three hours viewing the blurry, unknowable future
through the sharp, bright lens of the past. That's exactly three
hours more than any of your competitors are likely to invest in
thinking, learning, and planning. Like you and me, your
competitors are simply too busy to plan.

Do we have a deal?

Roy H. Williams

The Seven Laws
of the Advertising Universe

(Whence Cometh the Power of Ads to Work Magic)

An Energy of Words has existed since the day He said, "Let there be light." Learn how to use this energy. You are created in His image.

Masses of People are predictable, though an individual person is not. The exception does not disprove the rule.

Intellect and Emotion are partners who do not speak the same language. The intellect finds logic to justify what the emotions have decided. Win the hearts of the people, their minds will follow.

Time and Money are two sides of a single coin. No person gives you his money until he has first given you his time. Win the time of the people, their money will follow.

Sight and Sound function differently in the mind, with sound being the surer investment. Win the ears of the people, their eyes will follow.

Opportunity and Security are inversely proportionate. As one increases, the other must decrease. High returns are gained from low-risk strategies only through the passage of time. He who will cheat time must embrace the risk of failure.

Engage the Imagination, then take it where you will. Where the mind has repeatedly journeyed, the body will surely follow.
People go only to places they have already
been in their minds.

The Wizard of Ads

Turning Words into Magic and Dreamers into Millionaires

by Roy H. Williams

Bard Press
Austin, Texas

The Wizard of Ads
Turning Words into Magic and Dreamers into Millionaires

Bard Press
1515 Capital of Texas Highway S., Suite 205
Austin, TX 78746
512-329-8373 voice, 512-329-6051 fax
www.bardpress.com

Ordering Information
To order additional copies, contact your local bookstore or call 800-945-3132.
Quantity discounts are available.
ISBN 1-885167-29-6 trade paperback, 1-885167-32-6 hardcover

Library of Congress Cataloging-in-Publication Data

Williams, Roy H.
    The wizard of ads : turning words into magic and dreamers into millionaires / by Roy H. Williams.
        p.   cm.
    Includes index.
    ISBN 1-885167-32-6 (hc), 1-885167-29-6 (pbk)
    1. Advertising. 2. Small business.
HF5823.W497 1998
659.1--dc21   98-17430
                                   CIP

The author may be contacted at the following address:
Roy H. Williams
Williams Marketing, Inc.
1760 FM 967
Buda, TX 78610
512-295-5700 voice, 512-295-5701 fax
www.mondaymemo.com

Credits

Developmental editor: **Chris Maddock**
Editor: **Jeff Morris**
Proofreaders: **Deborah Costenbader, Clare Townes**
Index: **Linda Webster**
Cover design: **Hugh Pirnie**
Text design/production: **Jeff Morris**
Art direction: **Suzanne Pustejovsky**

First printing: May 1998
Second printing: October 1998
Third printing: December 1998

Contents

I. Turning Words into Magic

Advice on ◆ *trendcasting* ◆ *why good ads stick in your mind* ◆ *the qualitative trap* ◆ *being believable* ◆ *the quick set-up* ◆ *letting people live in fantasy* ◆ *pitfalls of price-driven ads* ◆ *predictability* ◆ *what you're really saying* ◆ *your reticular activator* ◆ *substantiation* ◆ *intellect vs. emotion* ◆ *and more...*

II. Turning Strangers into Customers

Thoughts on ◆ the delight factor ◆ passion ◆ the power of preconception ◆ your unique selling proposition ◆ initiative ◆ personality ◆ living in reality ◆ the benefits of failure ◆ the planning problem ◆ the power of presentation ◆ listening to idiots ◆ and much more...

III. Turning Dreams into Realities

Insights into ◆ *why you're so lucky* ◆ *the sad predominance of pessimism* ◆ *living a win-win life* ◆ *the power of dreams* ◆ *the importance of now* ◆ *the necessity of focus* ◆ *how to measure success* ◆ *how to recognize destiny* ◆ *knowing your own vision* ◆ *and still more…*

Part One

Turning Words into Magic

1

Nine Secret Words

EAN DOWN SO THAT I MAY SPEAK INTO YOUR EAR, for the thing I am about to tell you is not for the others to know. I share with you now the secret knowledge known to only a powerful few. I give you the Nine Words which, if held in your heart, will transform Success and Failure into mere coins that you may pull from your pocket and bestow upon those you would favor."

Leaning closer, I could feel his weak and ragged breath on my ear as he whispered:

"The risk of insult is the price of clarity."

Then he was gone.

I wish we could have spoken longer, for there were many other things I was forced to learn the hard way, but the old wizard was definitely right. The risk of insult is the price of clarity, and it is a price few are willing to pay.

To be clearly understood, one must speak the simple, essential truth as plainly as he is able. While many of those listening will say, "Such refreshing candor! So bold and direct!" others will say, "He is tactless, blunt, rude, insensitive, and unrefined."

Believe me, I know. While others debate the necessity of ruffling a few feathers, I'm usually in the backyard plucking the chicken. This always angers a handful of people, but most folks appreciate a fine chicken dinner.

Is clarity worth the risk of insult? Most people think not, and it is for this reason that most advertising is flaccid. Those who take the risk, however, will enjoy rewards far beyond a mere chicken dinner.

If in your advertising you are willing to speak the simple, essential truth as plainly as you are able, and if you are willing to support what you say with illustration and example, meet me in the backyard. We'll start with a chicken dinner and then we'll take over the world.

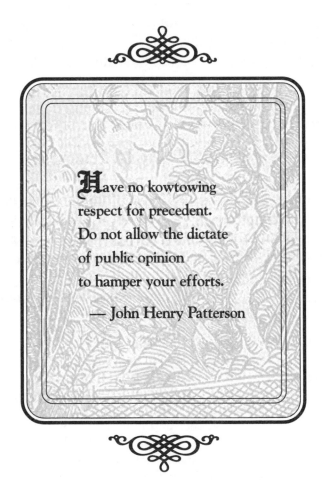

Have no kowtowing respect for precedent. Do not allow the dictate of public opinion to hamper your efforts.

— John Henry Patterson

2

Buried Treasure

I N THE BOOK *INFLUENCING HUMAN BEHAVIOR* you will find the following chapters:

1. The Key Problem: Capturing the Attention
2. The Appeal to Wants
3. The Problem of Vividness
4. The Psychology of Effective Speaking
5. The Psychology of Effective Writing
6. Crossing the Interest Deadline
7. Making Ideas Stick
8. Diagnosing the Public
9. The Technique of Humor

Would it surprise you to learn that this amazingly insightful book was written during the presidency of Calvin Coolidge by a man whose name you've never heard, yet the ideas put forward are significantly more advanced than most of what is being taught in advanced marketing today?

Writers of yesteryear did not have to worry about being politically correct; they simply blurted out the truth.

> The man who has nothing to offer the world that the world needs, should telephone the undertaker, for he is a dead one, whether he knows it or not.
>
> — Elbert Hubbard, *A Message to Ad-Men*, 1903

The person who can capture and hold attention is the person who can effectively influence human behavior. Who is a failure in life? Obviously, it is a person without influence; one to whom no one attends: the inventor who can persuade no one of the value of his device; the merchant who cannot attract enough customers into his store; the teacher whose pupils whistle or

stamp or play tricks while he tries to capture their attention; the poet who writes reams of verse which no one will accept.
— H. A. Overstreet, *Influencing Human Behavior*, 1925

Today's generation mistakenly assumes we know more about people than any previous generation. In reality, our minds today are mostly crammed with technology, entertainment, and news. Past generations occupied their minds less with technology and more with people. Five minutes in an old book quickly reveals that most of what is being sold today as new insights into human behavior is merely the rediscovery of knowledge we have had for centuries.

To learn things not yet rediscovered, you must read old books. There you will find the wisdom of your ancestors and the keys to your future. ♋

History must repeat itself because we pay such little attention to it the first time.

— Blackie Sherrod

3

Handy to Have Around

AVE YOU EVER NOTICED how the smartest people are always a little odd? This is because there's a fine line between genius and insanity. Isaac and John balance on this line like acrobats on a high wire. I consider them geniuses, but their more intimate friends think they're crazy. Maybe their friends are right.

Crazy people are handy to have around because they see things differently than the rest of us. They see connections the rest of us miss. It is this unusual ability to see the connections between seemingly unrelated ideas that has led to all of humankind's most important discoveries.

Isaac knows the planets circle the sun at a tremendous speed, but he cannot understand why they don't fly off into space. What is the string that keeps them tied to the sun?

At lunch one day, Isaac suddenly sees the invisible string as it pulls a piece of fruit toward the earth. "The planets are like this fruit," he thinks. "The sun is like the earth. The force that pulls the fruit toward the earth is the same invisible string that causes the planets to circle the sun instead of flying off into space." Isaac names the invisible string "gravity," and science takes a giant leap forward. The queen decides Isaac is a genius and dubs him Sir Isaac Newton.

John stares at the tool used by coinmakers to stamp images into metal and thinks, "Coinmakers have been using stamps like these since the time of Christ." Later he sees a winemaker hard at work, squeezing the juice from grapes in a winepress.

Suddenly he remembers the coinmaker's stamping tool. "What if I rubbed ink on the bottom of a coinmaker's stamp and attached it beneath the plate of a winepress? Instead of the image of the king, each coin stamp would bear a letter of the alphabet. Instead of grapes, there would be paper. . . ."

⟶ Before John Gutenberg, the Chinese were the technological leaders of the world. John's vision of the connection between the coin stamp and the winepress not only accelerated the Renaissance but sparked the Industrial Revolution and is largely responsible for today's European domination of the world.

While John is credited with the invention of the printing press, in reality he "invented" nothing. Coin stamps and winepresses had been in use since the time of Christ. John simply saw a connection.

Would you like to learn to see such connections? I'll do my best to teach you, but be warned: if ever you learn to do it, few will call you a genius.

Most will just say you're crazy. ❧

(handwritten margin note, rotated: "John Leaman, "Johann"")

Creative thinking is today's most prized profit-producing possession for any individual, corporation, or country. It has the capacity to change you, your business, and the world.

— Robert P. Crawford

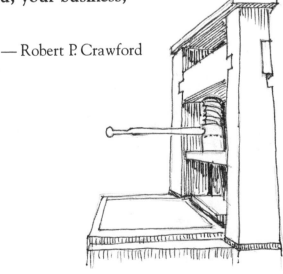

4

The Mousetrap Myth

I F A MAN CAN . . . make a better mousetrap than his neighbor . . . the world will make a beaten path to his door." So said Ralph Waldo Emerson.

Sorry, Ralph, but you were wrong. Forty-six years after you died, the better mousetrap was invented, and path beating did not occur.

In 1928, Chester M. Woolworth offered the world a much-improved mousetrap. It sold for twelve cents. The price of the older, less effective mousetrap, however, was only five cents. The better mousetrap failed.

What neither Emerson nor Woolworth realized is that once a mouse has been caught, most people dispose of both mouse and trap. No one wants to throw away a trap that costs two and a half times as much to replace. Even less does anyone wish to clean and reuse it.

We continue to buy the same mousetrap that was used during the lifetime of Ralph Waldo Emerson, even though dozens of superior mousetraps have since been invented. We buy the old ones because they work. We see no need for improvement.

Yet the power of Emerson's promise continues to lure thousands of inventors, each of whom stares dreamily toward the ceiling and whispers, "The world will beat a path to my door."

It has been quite some time since Emerson first painted his image of fame and recognition, and although his promise proved false, you and I still continue to recite the Better Mousetrap Myth because it is our hope that we might someday actually find the world beating a path to our door.

If nothing else, Emerson's maxim teaches us that words that conjure a pleasing image in the mind are words that will live forever. Suppose Emerson had said, "If you build a better mousetrap, there is a chance you will be able to sell it, but it will take a lot of hard work, and your mousetrap cannot cost more than the mousetrap it replaces." Would we have remembered this bit of wisdom for as long as we have?

Forget about a better mousetrap. Concentrate on better words. 🐍

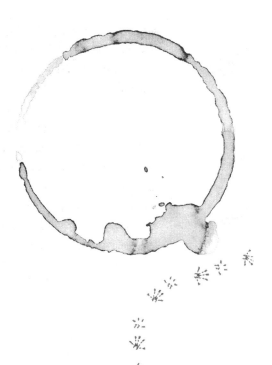

5

The Rest of the Mousetrap Story

HAVE ADVISED YOU not to pin your hopes on the magic of a better mousetrap, but to place your confidence in the power of better words. Let me amplify the point.

The adage that launched the Mousetrap Myth reads thus: "If a man can write a better book, preach a better sermon, or make a better mousetrap than his neighbor, though he build his house in the woods, the world will make a beaten path to his door."

Hundreds of sources readily confirm Ralph Waldo Emerson to be the author of these words, but no one can name the year he wrote them, nor the publication in which they appear. This is because the quote was actually penned twenty-eight years after Emerson died — by an ad writer named Elbert Hubbard. Trying to explain how his manufacturing company was able to attract large numbers of visitors to the tiny village of East Aurora, New York, Hubbard admits that he wrote the mousetrap epigram, then "gave it specific gravity by attributing it to one Ralph Waldo Emerson."

The Fra,
May 1911

Was Hubbard a liar? In my opinion, no. He merely told the truth a little more powerfully than what was completely accurate. You'll find the following on page 528 in volume 8 of Emerson's *Journal,* February 1855:

> Common Fame; I trust a good deal to common fame, as we all must. If a man has good corn, or wood, or boards, or pigs, to sell, or can make better chairs or knives, crucibles or church organs, than anybody else, you will find a broad, hard-beaten road to his house, though it be in the woods.

Hubbard said what Emerson said. Only Hubbard said it better.

We remember the words of Hubbard because, unlike Emerson, Hubbard used verbs that are visually active: "write," "preach," "make"; he gave us images that are clear: "book," "sermon," "mousetrap"; and his promise of benefit was memorable: ". . . the world will make a beaten path to his door."

Emerson's original statement is known to only the most diligent of researchers because it is neither active, clear, nor memorable: "I trust a good deal to common fame, as we all must." Emerson's images are cluttered and unfocused: corn, wood, boards, pigs, chairs, knives, crucibles, church organs; and the promise of benefit is soft, stumbling to its end with a qualifier: ". . . you will find a broad, hard-beaten road to his house, though it be in the woods."

Rather than closing as Emerson does, with the image of the house in the woods, Hubbard, an ad writer, leads us through his woods a bit earlier, so that he might close with a grand gesture — that unforgettable image of the whole world beating a path to our door.

Emerson may have had a profound idea, but it took the refinements of an ad writer to cause it to live forever in the imaginations of men.

How good is your ad writer? ❧

The advertising man is a liaison between the products of business and the mind of the nation. He must know both before he can serve either.

— Glenn Frank

6

Elevators Don't Read Minds

YOU STOP AT THE STOP SIGN, but your mind doesn't stop with you. The car on the cross street pulls away and disappears into the distance. You sit and wait for the sign to turn green. ←

I walk alone into an elevator and the door closes behind me. I wait and wait, but nothing happens. After a couple of minutes, I realize, "Elevators don't read minds. I have to push a button."

You and I have so much to remember that we often forget what we're doing. We are the unfortunate victims of overchoice: too much to do, too little time. The problem is nationwide.

I tell you this to remind you of something that most advertisers forget: the customer is seldom paying attention. She simply has too many other things to think about. When exposed to your ad, she knows it's there, the same way I know the elevator button is there. The problem is that she's not thinking about it.

Every beginner's solution is to put an "attention getter" into the ad. Bright colors, loud noises, exclamation marks, and crazy stunts are the sad little attention getters most often used. The effect on your beautiful customer is much the same as sneaking up behind her and shouting,

"WATCH OUT!"

Is this any way to start a romance?

Don't pretend you haven't done it — we all have!

I vote for seduction.

I'm not talking about using sex appeal in your ads. I'm talking about enticing the customer with a thought more interesting than the thought she's thinking. The skillful use of words is the most impressive of human powers.

The mind of the customer is a glorious thing. Every waking moment it is scanning, scanning, scanning the horizon for things of interest. The common, the mundane, the average, the predictable are ignored; the unusual, the intriguing, the fascinating are immediately spied and examined.

If your goal is to cause the customer to willingly give you her attention, isn't the solution obvious? You must offer her a thought more interesting than the thought that currently occupies her mind.

This does not require shouting. It requires art. ᖇ

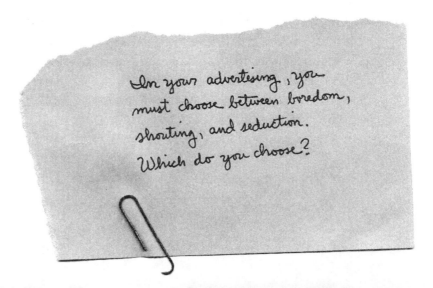

In your advertising, you must choose between boredom, shouting, and seduction. Which do you choose?

7

Pushing a Car

AVE YOU EVER HAD TO PUSH A CAR? Using your back and your legs and every ounce of strength you can summon, you gasp and strain and make faces as the doubt flickers through your mind: "I'm not sure I can do this." Then the car moves its first inch and you find strength you never knew you had. The second inch is slightly easier, but now you're thinking, "I'm not sure I can last." By the time you've moved it a yard, all doubts have fled. "Of course I can do this. I can do anything." Soon you're pushing just hard enough to keep the car rolling as you trot along behind it, basking in the applause of an imaginary crowd.

Launching an ad campaign is exactly like pushing a car.

I believe there are laws of the universe that cannot be cheated and that these laws apply in every area of our lives. One of these is the law of inertia. My dictionary defines inertia as "the tendency of all objects and matter in the universe to stay still if still, or, if moving, to go on moving in the same direction."

Your car doesn't begin to roll the moment you begin to push, and it doesn't stop rolling the moment you quit. The inertia that is your enemy at first becomes your ally in the end. Momentum is a wonderful thing, isn't it? But it never comes cheaply.

Likewise, advertising doesn't begin to work as quickly as you would like, but it also doesn't quit working until long after it has been abandoned. (Assuming, of course, that you ever got it rolling at all.)

So where are you now? Are you trotting along behind the car, providing the nudge it needs to keep rolling, or are you still pushing with all your strength in an attempt to pick up speed?

If ever you find yourself straining and doubting, call your ad man. He's been waiting his whole life for the chance to help you push that car. ᴄᴧ∾

$$F = d(mv)/dt$$

$$e = \frac{1}{2}mv^2$$

8

Home Movies

"THIS IS ME AT THE GRAND CANYON. This is me standing in front of Niagara Falls. This is me scuba diving in the Caribbean."

This is an idiot showing home movies.

The problem with home movies is never the content, but always the perspective. Scuba diving in the Caribbean is an adventure best experienced without some fool standing in front of the camera, telling you what he had for lunch or what he's about to do. (Now the whole family is waving at the camera, see?)

The genius of Jacques Cousteau is that he points the camera always at the underwater cave, the shark, the sunken ship — never at himself. We experience his undersea world and are hypnotized. Jacques takes us there.

You see only the tip of the canoe at the bottom of the screen, the smooth, swift river ahead. The current quickens and you hear a distant roar. The horizon draws near as the river shortens and the water grows more insistent. The roar now deafening, the current compelling, the tip of the canoe hangs for a moment in empty space, then tips sharply ninety degrees. You fall one hundred sixty-eight feet in an eternal three seconds. Suddenly the roar is gone and all light disappears with it. You are momentarily in absolute darkness. Now light reappears and grows slowly brighter as you rise gently toward the surface.

This is how Jacques Cousteau would show you Niagara Falls.

If you will write powerful advertising, you must point the movie camera of language to that place in the mind where you want the listener to go. The imagination can be a powerful thing, but only when the listener is a participant in your movie.

Bad advertising is like home movies. In your ads, please, never point the camera at yourself.

You're just not that interesting.

Horseshoe Falls from below, Niagara Falls

NF-35

9

The Important One Is "You"

OU'RE WRITING AN AD that needs to produce results. Your ad-writing teachers have taught you to say the name of the company at least seven times in every ad. Your experience tells you that cramming the name of the company into places where it wouldn't normally be heard will just make the ad sound like an ad.

You've wrestled with this problem, haven't you?

The teacher who taught you to say the name of the company at least seven times is probably the same teacher who taught you to use loud noises and sound effects as attention getters and that words like "discount" and "sale" are irresistible.

I won't call this teacher a fool, but I think he'll do nicely until a real fool comes along.

The most irresistible word in the English language has only three letters. The most powerful of all words is "you."

"You" engages the imagination of the listener. It puts the action of your spot in present tense active. Skillful use of the word "you" makes the listener a participant in your ad. Here's a sixty-second example:

> **Announcer:** You are standing in the snow five and one-half miles above sea level, gazing at a horizon hundreds of miles away. Life here is very simple. You live, or you die. No compromises, no whining, no second chances. This is a place constantly ravaged by wind and storm, where every ragged breath is an accomplishment. You stand on the uppermost pinnacle of the earth. This is the mountain they call Everest. Yesterday it was considered unbeatable. But that was yesterday.

No, its not S-E-X!

Client: As Edmund Hillary surveyed the horizon from the peak of Mount Everest, he monitored the time on a wristwatch that had been specifically designed to withstand the fury of the world's most angry mountain. Rolex believed Sir Edmund would conquer the mountain, and especially for him they created the Rolex Explorer.

Announcer: In every life, there is a Mount Everest to be conquered. When you have conquered yours, you'll find your Rolex waiting patiently for you to come and pick it up at Justice Jewelers, your official Rolex jeweler, on Highway 65 at Battlefield Road.

Client: I'm Woody Justice, and I've got a Rolex for you.

Did you hear the wind whistling past the microphone? Did you feel the awesome solitude? Were you proud to be standing on the pinnacle of the earth?

In this ad, you already own a Rolex that is "waiting patiently for you to come and pick it up." As a listener, you are inextricably engaged by the power of the imagery. By the end of this sixty-second radio ad, ownership of the watch has already been transferred. It all begins with "you." ❧

10
No Laughing Matter

OOD ADS ARE EITHER INTELLECTUAL (information focused) or emotional (experience focused). A well-written emotional ad causes the listener to imagine herself taking precisely the action you would like her to take: "As you step across the ancient, tree-filled lawn toward the torch-lit gates of the Plaza del Fuego, the cares of the day melt into forgetfulness as you anticipate the evening ahead. There is no finer meal to be had on earth. There is no place quite like this one."

When the decision to be made is not an emotional one, however, your ad must instead appeal to the intellect. And an intellectual ad is no laughing matter.

Most people write intellectual ads the same way they tell a joke. They open with an obscure reference to what's coming, then add relevant data little by little, working their way up to the punch line. This is the worst possible way to write an ad. An ad is not a joke. Those listening to a joke are committed to listening. Those listening to an ad are not.

Bad intellectual ads begin with a setup, wherein the writer tries to set the stage for the argument he plans to make. As these ads drone on, the customer thinks, "Get to the point. Blurt it out. Tell me plainly what's in it for me." In less than seven seconds, the customer stops listening entirely.

A bad intellectual ad may take fifteen seconds or more to get to the point. Worse still, when the point is finally made, it usually answers a question no one is asking.

A good intellectual ad begins by delivering a punch line directly to a felt need, then quickly substantiating any claims made during the opening statement. Today's public prefers that you prove what you say.

Intellectual or emotional, a good ad is a satisfying experience. Are your ads satisfying, or are they a joke? ꙮ

11

Look for the Loophole!

OST ADS ARE FULL OF LOOPHOLES.

"Roy, I'm way ahead of you on this one. I always look for the loophole, and I usually find it. Loopholes are the reason I ignore most advertising."

Yes, I know you're good at spotting the loophole, because so is everyone else.

If you want your advertising to be more productive, you need to quit looking for the loopholes in other people's ads and start looking for the loopholes in your own.

A persuasive intellectual ad begins with a frank statement of benefit, then quickly substantiates every claim. Closing loopholes is the difference between merely informing the customer and persuading her. Below is an example of a persuasive intellectual ad (with the customer's thoughts in parentheses).

Parkins and Maddock will cut the cost of your insurance by least 10 percent

(Or what?)

or buy you dinner at the Plaza del Fuego.

(I'm not sitting through a two-hour sales pitch just for a lousy dinner.)

All it takes is a three-minute phone call, and there's no one you have to meet.

(Still too much of a hassle. I don't know the details of my coverage.)

So the next time you reach in your mailbox and pull out the insurance renewal, walk straight to the phone and call Parkins and Maddock. Read them the limits and deductibles printed on the notice

(That's right! The renewal notice has the details of my coverage on it.)

and they will immediately name the price at which they can give you identical coverage, apples for apples.

(Identical coverage? No one to meet? Just three minutes?)

If the Parkins and Maddock price isn't at least ten percent lower, you're off to the Plaza del Fuego.

(I've always wanted to go to the Plaza del Fuego.)

You're going to have to write someone a check. Why not write a smaller one to Parkins and Maddock?

(I need to remember to call these people when I get my renewal notice.)

If Parkins and Maddock were patient and gave this ad sufficient repetition, it would keep their telephones dancing across their desktops month after month, year after year. Unfortunately, the ad below is the one you're more likely to hear.

For more than fifty years, hundreds of families have trusted their insurance needs to the caring professionals at Parkins and Maddock

(Why?)

because competitive pricing is a Parkins and Maddock specialty

("Competitive?" Doesn't that mean "about the same price as everyone else"?)

and they are known for their fast, fair, and friendly service.

(Yeah, until you have a claim.)

So when you need auto, home, health, life, or any other type of insurance

 (I just love talking about insurance.)

find out how much Parkins and Maddock can save you by calling them

 (Is that softball game tonight or tomorrow night?)

at 862-3791.

 (I think I'll stop and get a Coke.)

That number again is 862-3791.

 (And maybe some fries. I love french fries.)

Parkins and Maddock is open weekdays till seven for your convenience

 (I think that game is tomorrow night.)

and until four on Saturdays, but closed on Sundays.

 (But I'd better call and check on it.)

Find out for yourself why hundreds of families

 (Should I take a burger home for Bobby?)

trust Parkins and Maddock, year after year.

 (Yeah, a burger with cheese.)

Call Parkins and Maddock today at 862-3791.

 (I'll get myself one, too.)

You'll be glad you did.

 (But without the cheese.)

See the difference? ⌘

12

When the Truth Is Not Persuasive

 KNOW IT WILL SHOCK YOU TO HEAR THIS, but telling the truth is rarely persuasive. This unfortunate fact has caused many businesses owners to invent a whole new language of deceit. This language is often excused as "advertising."

Deceitful advertising is common today because the honest business people of yesterday assumed all they had to do was "tell the truth" about their superior products. The result, all too often, was a dramatic loss of business to competitors who used deceitful advertising to sell inferior goods. With his family's future on the line, the reluctant response of the honest business person was often to fight fire with fire.

Anyone who believes in this philosophy has obviously never tried to put out a fire. The tragic result of "fighting fire with fire" has been a nationwide inferno of deceitful advertising. "If the public won't buy it for $20, we'll mark it $40 and sell it for half price!"

These business owners knew they couldn't fool all the people all the time, but they were able to make a nice income fooling some of the people some of the time. Now these business owners are frightened because it's getting harder to fool any of the people any of the time.

The real tragedy is that so many honest business people abandoned the truth in their advertising. You see, it wasn't the truth that was ineffective. The mistake was in assuming it was enough simply to tell it. If you want the truth to prevail, you must cause people to *realize* the truth. This requires much more skill than is required to simply tell it.

Honest persuasion is the water that will put out any fire. ❧

Truth we are told is truth we may not accept; the truth we have realized is the only truth we own.

13

Velcro, the Ad Writer's Friend

T HE GOAL OF ADVERTISING is for your message to hold tightly to the brain. Most advertising does not. Do you want the public to remember your ads? The secret is Velcro.

George de Mestral discovered the secret of memorable advertising in 1941 in the Jura Mountains of France. After a day of hunting, scrambling through woods and brush, he found his wool pants covered with burrs. No matter how he tried to remove them, those little burrs were on his pants to stay. Fascinated by their tenacity, George inspected them under a magnifying glass and found that each of them had hundreds of tiny hooks engaged in the loops of his woolen fabric.

George made a machine to duplicate the hooks and loops using nylon. He called his new product VELCRO®, from the French words VELours and CROchet. The rough side of Velcro is made of tiny, flexible hooks; the fuzzy side, small, soft loops.

Therein lies the secret of memorable advertising. What is the brain but a surface covered with trillions of tiny, flexible hooks? What is memorable advertising but a series of words, sounds, or mental images covered with small, soft loops?

You must cover your ads with small, soft loops, but it's not as simple as it seems. Have you ever noticed how some pieces of Velcro hold much tighter than others? George de Mestral found that randomly oriented loops offer much greater holding power than loops arranged in neat rows. The more unpredictable the loops, the stronger the bond. Neatly arranged loops have little holding power.

When ad writers present their clients' information in a predictable manner or use predictable words, they are making orderly loops. The advertiser may like the ad because it is accurate and positive. But such ads have weak Velcro; they are forgettable.

The human mind discounts the predictable. When you see the punch line coming, the joke is never funny. There can be no curiosity where there is no mystery, no delight without surprise.

When you understand the Velcro of the mind, you are halfway to fame and fortune. The only thing you need now is a mental trigger. But we'll talk about that in another chapter. ◞

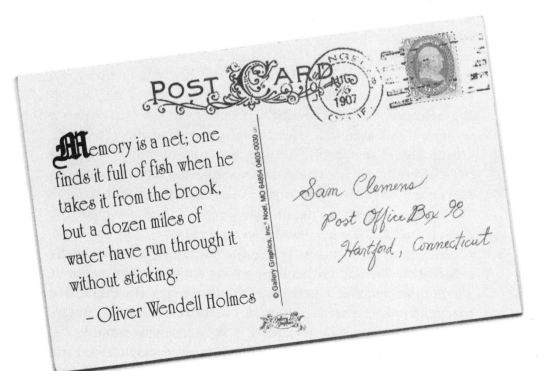

POST CARD

AUG 26 1907

Memory is a net; one finds it full of fish when he takes it from the brook, but a dozen miles of water have run through it without sticking.

– Oliver Wendell Holmes

© Gallery Graphics, Inc.® Noel, MO 64854 0403-0030

Sam Clemens
Post Office Box 98
Hartford, Connecticut

14
Reaching the Right People

DVERTISING BEGAN TO DETERIORATE the day we let the scientific types get involved. Now don't get me wrong, I think there is a place for every type of person, but scientific types should stick with things scientific.

Unfortunately, someone forgot to lock the door one day and a scientific type slipped in and said, "The secret to more effective advertising would be to reach the right people."

I wish I had been there. I would have casually turned to him and said, "It's not who you reach, it's what you say, stupid," and ended the whole thing right there. But I wasn't in the room. And since he was a scientific type and his idea made sense, everyone began walking in circles, mindlessly parroting, "Reach the right people. Reach the right people."

The problem is that advertising is not scientific. Trying to "reach the right people" usually leads to overtargeting and overconfidence. It has caused more stupid mistakes, frustration, and failures than any other myth in the history of commerce.

It begins when the advertising salesperson says, "I've got the right people," and since you believe this is what matters most, you buy what he's selling. When the campaign fails, you don't consider the possibility that your ad was not persuasive or that it was not given enough repetition. You simply say, "He didn't have the right people after all." You blame the radio station for having "the wrong kind of listener," the direct mail company for "having a bad list," and the billboard company for giving you "the wrong locations."

American business owners are frustrated with their advertising because they keep trying to make it a science. Advertising is *not* a science. The assumption that an advertising salesperson can give you exclusive access to a particular group of people is simply ridiculous. Every American is reached by multiple vehicles of advertising every day. Having the right message is what matters.

It's not who you reach, it's what you say.

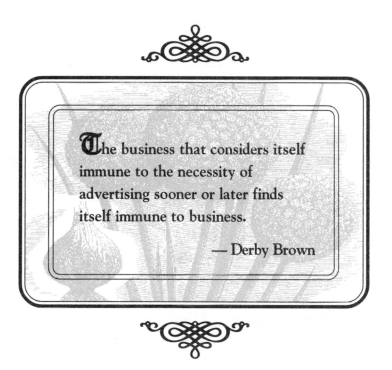

The business that considers itself immune to the necessity of advertising sooner or later finds itself immune to business.

— Derby Brown

15
All I Said Was . . .

 MAKE A SIMPLE STATEMENT: "It's not who you reach, it's what you say that makes the difference."

But you should see the anxiety! First the startled eyebrows and slackened jaw. Then, almost imperceptibly, the eyebrows descend and the chin moves slowly upward until dawning realization becomes clearly visible discomfort. Angry thoughts now gather like storm clouds behind the eyes as the words of rebuttal are chosen. Finally, the eyes are slits and the jaw is tight. "Do you mean to say . . ." is then followed by an absurd example obviously meant to put me in my place.

This is my most difficult moment. If I modify my statement or weaken it, you can be sure that I've done the listener no good. His religion of "reaching the right people" is so deeply ingrained that he will do virtually anything to justify his continued belief in it. If I am honest and say, "Of course it matters a little," he will continue on his search for The Right People like a knight on his quest for the Holy Grail. Upon finding The Right People, he will triumphantly deliver to them his weak and unconvincing message.

I've got to make him understand the overwhelming importance of saying the right thing. So I resort to overstatement.

The truth is that it does matter who you reach. It's just that finding the right people is ridiculously simple. I've never once met an advertiser whose failure was due to reaching the wrong people. Yet I can name countless instances where miracles were wrought through a simple change in message. These advertisers were already reaching the right people. They just weren't saying the right thing.

The attraction of The Right People is that they are easily identifiable and quantifiable. Searching for The Right People lets an advertiser design his ad campaign with all the confidence of a vacationer studying a road map.

"Saying the right thing" is an altogether different issue. In this, there are no rules, no road maps, no intellectual evidence. No way to justify why you did what you did when things don't turn out as you planned.

Most advertisers cling to their religion of "reaching the right people," because acknowledging their inability to say the right thing makes them feel incapable and uncomfortable.

Frankly, it scares the hell out of them.

16

The Mental Trigger

OU BUY A NEW CAR. As soon as you drive out of the dealer's lot, you begin seeing cars just like yours everywhere you go. We can safely assume these cars were here yesterday — but yesterday you didn't notice them, and today you aren't looking for them. What's happening?

Your old refrigerator begins to make odd noises. You finish breakfast and go to work, immediately forgetting about the refrigerator and the noise. During lunch you read the paper and notice an ad for refrigerators on sale. You weren't thinking about your refrigerator, but you notice the ad anyway. What's happening?

You are asked to total fourteen different columns of single-digit numbers. Each of the fourteen columns adds up to exactly fourteen. You are now asked to name a vegetable. You say "carrots." Why?

Planting a reticular activator in the mind of the customer is the Mount Everest of ad writers. The reticular activator is a mental trigger in your unconscious that directs your attention and causes you to notice and remember things you never intentionally committed to memory. Successfully implanted, a reticular activator will cause your prospective customer immediately to think of your company when she has need of your product.

It is easier to implant a reticular activator using sound rather than sight. Medical science tells us it takes 29 percent longer to understand written words than spoken words. This is because the brain must translate the written word into the spoken word before it can be understood. When we memorize the written word, it is the *sound* of the words we remember, not their appearance on the page. This is true even when we have been reading silently. We hear the words in our minds.

The eye cannot be trusted to remember what it has seen. One of the most frustrating parts of police work is that different eyewitnesses often recall an event differently. Yet people can repeat the last sentence a person said, even if they weren't paying attention. How often has someone asked, "Are you listening?" and even though you weren't, you could repeat verbatim their last statement?

Information taken in through the eyes enters into iconic memory and disappears in less than one second. Information that enters through the ears rattles around in echoic memory for nearly five seconds before it dissipates.

Well-written, intrusive ads establish echoic retention through the use of a reticular activator. Echoic retention and a reticular activator will cause you to say "carrots" after repeating the number "fourteen."

How many times have you heard the phrase "fourteen-karat gold"? ◈

17
Furnishings of the Mind

THE HUMAN MIND is a crowded room, overflowing with too many memories of smell and color, taste and touch, sight and sound. Half-remembered words and buried emotions lie stacked, layer upon layer, in piles that grow deeper with each passing year.

A familiar face, a special place, a bit of a song, a distinctive smell — familiar touchstones like these bring order to the chaos and remind us of who we are and why we do the things we do. Such sensory memories are like old friends; each encounter with one of them brings our self-image more sharply into focus.

Advertising arrives as an uninvited guest, pounding on the door of the overcrowded mind. The subconscious, that wary gatekeeper, asks, "Who do you know? Name any friends you may have in this room." The ad that associates itself with a familiar touchstone immediately gains entrance into the mind. The ad that stands alone is just as quickly dismissed. "Go away," says the subconscious. "It's too crowded in here for you."

Things that are new and unknown are more quickly accepted when related to the known and familiar. Do your ads touch the familiar in your customers' lives? Do people relate to the things you say? Or are you merely droning on about Who, What, When, and Where, while failing to answer the pivotal question: Why?

Most ads are written under the assumption that the customer is asking, "Who are you? What is your product? When are you open? Where are you located?" Unfortunately, the customer's only real question is "Why should I care?"

Your customer is saying, "Tell me a story that has *me* in it. Don't tell me a story about you. What's in it for me? Can you save me time, make me money, reduce stress in my life, or cause people to think more highly of me? If not, then leave me alone. You're wasting my time."

Most ads are about the product or the company that makes it. Such ads yield disappointing results. The best ads are about the customer and how the product will change his life.

What are your ads about? ❧

18
Selling to Walter Mitty

HE WORLD LOOKS AT YOU and sees one person; you look in the mirror and see another.

This odd difference between reality and self-image was memorably illustrated by Miguel de Cervantes in 1605. Don Quixote saw himself as a chivalrous knight and protector of the fair maiden Dulcinea. The world around him saw only a weary old man and a servant girl.

"What giants?" said Sancho Panza.

"Those you see there," answered his master, "with the long arms, and some have them nearly two leagues long."

"Look, your worship," said Sancho. "What we see there are not giants but windmills, and what seem to be their arms are the vanes that turn by the wind and make the millstone go."

"It is easy to see," replied Don Quixote, "that you are not used to this business of adventures."

Three hundred thirty-seven years later, it is James Thurber's Walter Mitty who, in the space of a single afternoon, is the commander of a navy hydroplane, a life-saving surgeon, an expert marksman, and an intrepid army captain. Walter Mitty isn't crazy. He just has trouble convincing the outside world of who he is inside.

"The Secret Life of Walter Mitty" is a favorite American story because it speaks to the Mitty in each of us. Who among us has never played cowboy, astronaut, princess, or nurse? Like Don and Walter, each of us has a secret life, and it is silly to pretend that our outward choices are not influenced by the people we are inside.

If we insist on intellectual honesty, we must urge Don and Walter to abandon their childish dreams. But if we would sell our

Drawing by James Thurber

product and make two customers happy, we will speak not to a tired old man and a henpecked husband, but will eloquently address the needs of a chivalrous knight and an intrepid army captain.

It's called "advertising." ◿

There are two worlds: the world that we can measure with line and rule, and the world that we feel with our hearts and imagination.

— Leigh Hunt

19

Our Need for Definition

HO AM I, AND WHAT AM I DOING HERE?" is the oldest and perhaps most universal question of humankind. We all have a need to define who we are and where we fit in. My author friend, Richard Exley, says we have "a need to belong." This powerful need for definition is rarely discussed, but it is nonetheless universal, and an ability to tap into it is often the genesis of a very compelling ad campaign.

Our need for definition influences what we drive, where we live, how we furnish our homes, the clothes we wear, the clubs we join, the magazines we read, and the cola we drink.

As I have said many times, effective advertising must speak to a felt need. It has become my conviction that our need for definition is perhaps the most compelling need felt by individuals in our society today. Most of our purchases involve self-expression, and we tend to buy things with which we identify. Let me give you an example.

I recently mailed a promotional piece to several hundred companies in targeted industries. One of the men who responded was the chairman of Ravenswood, a California vineyard. Mr. Foster sent me his very elegant, vertical business card, which ends with the statement "No Wimpy Wines."

My bond with Mr. Foster was immediate. Any man whose goals include a desire to avoid "wimpiness" in all its deviant forms is my kind of guy! I had noticed Ravenswood on the wine lists of most of the better restaurants, but I'd never tried it. Care to guess which wine is my new favorite? Yep, Ravenswood.

In some small way, I feel connected with Mr. Foster's Ravenswood, and even though the connection is small, it's far more than I have with any other winery. Mr. Foster was audacious enough to print "No Wimpy Wines" on his business cards, and it gained him a customer. Perhaps there are many other wines that are equally good, but I'll probably always be a Ravenswood man.

Like me, all of humankind has this need for definition, and the most powerful brands are those that help the customer define his identity.

Do you think I'm crazy? Trust me, every customer you have is just as crazy. Get in step with the lunacy, and watch your sales skyrocket. ❧

We are more easily persuaded, in general, by the reasons we ourselves discover than by those which are given to us by others.

— Blaise Pascal

20

The Cocaine of Advertising

SK YOUR PHYSICIAN HOW TO FEEL GOOD, and he'll look you squarely in the eye and say, "Eat right and exercise." Yet for every dollar spent in fitness centers, Americans spend nineteen dollars on cocaine. The reason? Two seconds after you snort cocaine you feel like Superman. Two weeks of diet and exercise just makes you hungry and sore.

The desire for instant gratification is harmless enough if the only thing it leads you to do is pay higher prices at a convenience store. But heaven help you if you demand instant gratification from your advertising! The business person looking for a financial quick fix will soon discover the cocaine of advertising, a four-letter magic chant:

SALE! SALE! SALE! SALE!

Good advertising is painful at first because you don't see immediate results. The impatient business owner will usually snort a little ad cocaine and then get defensive about it: "How can this be bad for me? I've never done better!" But just as the junkie never stops to consider how the drug is destroying his physical health, the business owner never stops to consider how "Sale! Sale! Sale!" undermines his business health. The first dose of cocaine makes him feel great. So does the next one, and the next, and the next — though it takes larger and larger doses to get the same effect. Therefore, it's almost impossible to convince the addict he has a problem, even though he started with only "Twenty Percent Off" and has now progressed to "Half Price."

Successful companies don't spend their ad dollars training their customers to wait for a sale. Do you? ◆

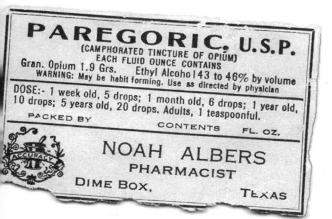

21
The World's Best Traffic Builder

I'D LIKE TO DO A TRAFFIC BUILDER. Do you know how to do a traffic builder? I think a good traffic builder is what we need."

One traffic builder, coming right up!

My favorite traffic builder involves three actors in police uniforms. The first "policeman" stands in the street in front of your business and diverts all traffic into your parking lot, where the second cop waves the cars into parking spaces. The third cop stands at the front door and blows his whistle to direct people into your store. When the place is fully packed, the faux gendarmes then yank off their uniforms and scurry in to begin selling customers.

Need any other good ideas?

There's a chance my traffic builder is slightly more stupid than yours, but only because mine is illegal. The traffic would be no less qualified than the crowd brought in by most other traffic-building schemes.

"Yes, I'm here because of the inflatable pink gorilla on your roof and the free hot dogs you talked about on the radio. Gosh, now that I see you're a car dealer, I suddenly have the urge to buy a new car!"

Running an ad under the pretense that "it's a good traffic builder" is from the same school of thought that says there's value in "getting your name out." If you're running for public office, getting your name out may be enough to get you elected, but if you want your ad to be remembered when the prospect has need of your product, you've got to have something attached to your name.

If a traffic builder helps reinforce your market position or communicate your unique selling proposition, it's much more than a mere traffic builder: it's a good ad that just happens to generate immediate traffic. Unfortunately, this kind of traffic is never predictable. An ad that creates good traffic one week may generate none the next.

These are your options: you can (1) write meaningful ads that will be remembered when the prospect has need of your product, or you can (2) write ads to bring in immediate traffic.

If you choose option 2, I know someone who can help you. His name is Oscar Meyer. He works with a pink gorilla. ᕤ

22

Reading Between the Lines

HAT'S A REALLY GREAT TOUPEE you're wearing. Where did you get it?"

"I've always liked pants like those. Are they coming back in style?"

"Are you always this funny when you're drunk?"

Even though the speakers didn't actually say to you, "That toupee isn't fooling anyone, those pants are out of style, and you talk like a drunk," you'd probably find it hard to respond warmly to these "compliments," because you would have heard more than was actually said.

Let me give you another example. I'm always flattered to meet people who say to me, "I really enjoy your articles!" but I've concluded from these meetings that my physical appearance must be somehow disappointing, because each of these people will invariably look me over, then ask, "Do you write them yourself?"

I guess my "college professor" look isn't working, because people seem to see me as just another bald guy with glasses and a beard. "And how did you meet your wife?" (Pennie is gorgeous.)

Like me, all of America has learned to hear much more than is spoken, especially when it comes to advertising. I'm convinced it was the glut of "hype" advertising that taught America to listen with suspicious ears. "Sale! Sale! Sale! 60%! 70%! Up to 80% Off! Save BIG during Dollar Buster Happy Daze!" This type of advertising worked well during the days of America's naiveté, but that day ended when we heard our first pitch from a multilevel marketing company or received our first letter from a time-share resort:

You have definitely won one of the following five prizes: (1) A Cadillac Eldorado (2) A Sport Boat (3) A $10,000 Savings Bond (4) His and Hers Motorcycles (5) A Rolex Watch. Please call to let us know when you can pick up your prize. Bring proof of identification.

To advertise effectively in today's America, we must understand our listeners' reluctance to believe the claims of advertising. We must *volunteer* the proof they need. Loud music, brightly colored balloons, and enthusiastic recitations of worn-out clichés will no longer convince people they are receiving good value. (Okay, there are still a few idiots out there, but the number grows smaller every day.)

The time has come when we must offer a product or service that is demonstrably better. It is no longer enough simply to tell bigger lies in a louder voice than the next guy. If you want your advertising to be productive, you must have a story to tell, and you must tell it persuasively.

By the way, a friend of mine got that time-share letter and took a day of vacation to travel 150 miles and pick up his prize. After subjecting him (unsuccessfully) to a relentless, two-hour sales pounding, his hosts tossed him a three-dollar inflatable raft and said, "Thanks for making the trip, Sport. Here's your boat."

You ask how I can be certain America is no longer naive? The time-share people quit mailing those letters only when the letters quit working. When was the last time you took a day of vacation to go pick up a new boat, Sport? ❧

23

Big Talk and Little Acorns

 EMEMBER THE STORY OF CHICKEN LITTLE? Sitting under an oak, he is beaned by a falling acorn and spends the rest of the afternoon running from one barnyard animal to another screaming, "The sky is falling! The sky is falling!"

In the original story, Chicken Little simply makes a laughable mistake. But let's suppose Chicken Little's friends repeatedly warn him about falling acorns. They tell him it's the peak season for acorns and gravity. But Chicken Little insists upon sitting under the tree anyway. And the acorn descends, just as predicted.

Now Chicken Little's Paul Revere act becomes a little irritating, doesn't it?

I have consulted a dozen Chicken Littles. They always say they want to experience "the kind of advertising that gets results," but they're never prepared for the actual experience. Though I warn them that powerful advertising will generate negative fallout from many sources, they answer, "Bring it on," then back-pedal vigorously as soon as a few people say, "I hate your ads."

Do you have the courage of your convictions? Are you ready to defend what you say? Or will you pound your chest like King Kong, then run like Peter Cottontail at the first sign of adversity?

Some of my best and most compelling ads never made the airwaves. These favorite campaigns were shot down by the spouse, the partner, the next-door neighbor, or some other well-meaning friend of the client, and the word, statement, or phrase that had to be eliminated was usually the most powerful line in the ad. The result of this "editing" is emasculated advertising. My success as an advertising consultant is owed to those clients who hear the sound of bombs and warfare all around them and shout, "Damn the torpedoes, full speed ahead!"

There is no plan so brilliant that it cannot be made utterly ineffective through compromise. "Yes, I can soften the ad. I can soften it so that it offends no one, says nothing, and sounds just like every other ad on the air. Please don't hold me responsible when the ad doesn't work. On second thought, perhaps the right thing for you to do is get out the yellow pages and look under 'A' for 'Advertising Agencies.' Let us know how this turns out."

Despite what you're thinking, my goal in writing this chapter was not to vent my frustration but to get you to examine the depth of your own convictions. What do you stand for? Are you willing to stand firm? Your answers to these two questions will determine the power and success of your advertising. ❧

Courage is a special kind of knowledge:
the knowledge of how to fear what ought
to be feared and how not to fear what
ought not to be feared.

— David Ben-Gurion

24

"No one goes there anymore. It's too crowded."

OME STATEMENTS MAKE NO SENSE AT ALL but are accepted as gospel anyway. A good example is the title of this essay, a comment purportedly made by Yogi Berra, whose command of the absurd is legendary.

Yogi often displays an insight into the obvious:

"You can observe a lot by just watching."

"When you come to a fork in the road, take it."

"If you can't imitate him, don't copy him."

"A nickel ain't worth a dime anymore."

"Business is fabulous, but my customers complain they hear my ads too much."

Okay, that last one wasn't Yogi. It was a client of mine, and he wasn't trying to be funny. Actually, a lot of my clients hear complaints about their ads from their customers. As you might expect, it's always the most successful clients.

Isn't it strange that although people complain bitterly that they hear an ad too often, no one ever complains of *reading* an ad too often? I commonly recommend radio and television, but rarely newspaper: "You can close your eyes but you can't close your ears."

You hear even when you're not listening, but you don't see unless you're watching. This is why you can sing hundreds of songs you never intended to learn, but you can't name the color of the car that sits in the driveway just five houses down the street from your home, even though you drive past it several times a week.

There are only two kinds of ads: echoic (sound) and iconic (sight). Echoic ads are far more intrusive than iconic ads. It is because of the intrusive nature of sound that people often complain about ads on the radio, but never about those in print.

The problem with using sound is that echoic ads require intense repetition to be effective. The reader of an iconic (print) ad can choose to study the fine print or read an ad multiple times, but she can also choose not to read it at all. The listener to an echoic ad is not allowed this control. She cannot hear your ad a second, third, or fourth time unless you decide she should.

To gain the miraculous results that echoic advertising offers, you must repeat your ads relentlessly. As Yogi says, "If people aren't complaining about your ads, you must be doing something wrong." (Okay — I lied about it being Yogi Berra. But it's true, anyway.) ❧

25

"But it's a *dry* heat."

T SURE IS HOT HERE IN ARIZONA!"

"Yes, but it's a ___ _____ ."

If you had three guesses to finish the sentence above, you could do it and have two guesses left over, right? The answer is predictable.

Predictability. It's what makes advertising sound like advertising, and it's one of the biggest reasons ad campaigns fail. Mouthing meaningless clichés, making unsubstantiated claims, and mindlessly assuming the customer is willing to believe whatever is said are the classic mistakes of advertisers across America.

Most advertisers want their ads to be "smooth," "polished," "professional," and "clever." Unfortunately, the public no longer trusts "smooth," "polished," "professional," or "clever" advertising. You know you've written a good ad when it doesn't sound like an ad.

Face it, your competitor believes most of the same things about his business that you believe about yours, and you're both trying to lead the customer to the same conclusion. You'll probably make the same claims, use the same logic, and offer the same assurances in your advertising. The problem is, the customer has heard it all before and doesn't believe either of you! To be persuasive, your ads must be frank, direct, and believable.

Your ad is believable only when the listener agrees with it. So how do you make the listener agree with you? Tell her what she already knows or suspects! Remind her of things you know she has experienced. Tell her her perceptions are accurate, and she'll probably agree with whatever you have to say. (Anyone who agrees with her can't possibly be wrong!)

Build on the foundation of a common perspective. Try to see your customer's needs as she sees her needs. Look at your product through her eyes, and you may discover how to speak to her felt needs. Walk a mile in her shoes before you talk to her about how her feet feel. ❧

26

Walking into Darkness

WHEN YOU WALK INTO A PITCH-DARK ROOM, your first instinct is always to turn on the light. But wouldn't you prefer the room to be well lit when you entered? Of course you would.

Then please explain why we leave these incredibly inconsiderate phone messages for each other that say nothing more than "Have him call me."

In effect, "Have him call me" says, "Tell him I want him to be ready for anything. I won't give him the courtesy of telling him how to prepare for our conversation." Returning this kind of phone call feels very much like walking into a dark room. Am I the only person who hates this?

Like good telephone etiquette, good advertising never asks the customer to walk into darkness. A good ad will describe in detail exactly what the customer can expect when he arrives at your place of business.

No person takes action until he has seen himself taking such action in his mind. We always imagine doing a thing before we do it. Causing your prospective customer to imagine a visit to your store is the highest goal of advertising. A good ad artfully describes what awaits the customer.

Do your ads enticingly describe what awaits your customer? Do your words create a series of mental pictures? To be effective, your ads must cause the customer to "see" himself doing what you want him to do. If you're patient and persistent, he will someday transfer this imagined experience into actual experience. He will finally do what he has "seen" himself do so many times.

The longer you keep it up, the better it works. Conversely, the style of advertising that whips the customer into immediate action works less and less well the longer you continue it. Do you have the patience to invest in doing it right? Can you write ads that will create the required series of mental images? If you cannot, find someone who can.

It is both classy and considerate to tell a receptionist what you would like to discuss with the boss. It is both classy and profitable to describe to your customer what he will experience the moment he steps through your door. No one likes walking into darkness. ෨

27

Hardwood, Hammer, and Nail

THE MIND OF YOUR PROSPECTIVE CUSTOMER is like a seasoned piece of hardwood. Your message is like a nail. The rhythmic strokes of the hammer represent the number of times your message — your unique selling position (USP) — is heard by the prospect.

Sleep is the hammer's claw. (Sleep: God's gift to the human race, purging our minds of the noise of the day. Sleep: The eraser of all advertising.)

Your goal is to drive the nail through the board and then clench it on the other side. Messages that are clenched are remembered for a lifetime. Tap, tap goes the hammer. But during the night the claw pulls the nail back out of its little hole! The following day you find nothing more than a faint indentation in the board. The nail is no longer in it. Your message is forgotten.

Using the hole you started the previous day, you position the nail again. Tap, tap goes the hammer. But again falls the veil of darkness, eyes close, and the claw does its work once more. Day after day, this scene is repeated; but ever so slowly, the hole gets deeper.

Driving the nail of your USP into the hardwood of the mind is like climbing a muddy mountain: three steps forward, two steps back, over and over again.

The frustration is simply too much. You believe advertising should pay off immediately! "It must be time to change the USP, because this one doesn't seem to be working."

But to change your USP is to start a new nail in a completely different spot on the board. The hole in which you have invested is now wasted. Why do you do this? Do you think there's a soft spot on the board somewhere? There is not. You can sharpen the nail (with better writing), but there are no soft spots on the board. Stay with the hole you've started!

Sharpen the nail.

Press on. Nothing in the world can take the place of persistence.

— Ray Kroc

28

A Time for True Lies

THERE ARE CERTAIN INDIVIDUALS who always seem to shout for perfect accuracy in advertising. But when emotions are involved, can there be such a thing as black-and-white certainty? The unique ability to tell the truth a little more powerfully than what is completely accurate is a skill that has long been used in places far beyond the field of advertising.

Three of the most famous statues in the world were sculpted inaccurately, on purpose, so that they might more accurately communicate reality.

Myron's *Discus Thrower* shows us a majestic athlete in mid-throw, except that from such a posture no athlete could ever expect to throw a discus more than a few feet (in reality, he'd be lucky not to fall over). Yet the *Discus Thrower* has been one of the world's most beloved sculptures for more than fifteen hundred years. You've never seen a truly accurate sculpture of a man throwing a discus, because every artist knows it would be a monumentally boring piece of art.

The Thinker, by Auguste Rodin, reveals a man lost in deep contemplation, except that Rodin shows us this "thinker" with his right elbow resting on his left knee — a very uncomfortable and unnatural position for anyone trying to concentrate. It's unlikely that any human in the history of the world has ever chosen to sit naked in such an uncomfortable position while working out his problems.

Even the great Michelangelo sculpted the head of his immortal *David* too large for the body because Michelangelo, like Rodin and Myron, knew that artistic exaggeration was utterly essential to the realistic portrayal of the human drama.

Does the great Norman Rockwell illustrate the real America on the cover of the *Saturday Evening Post*, or does he show us America as it ought to be, an America that each of us sees ever in our hearts, though never with our eyes?

If it sounds like I'm trying to defend the highly criticized practice of overstatement in the fine art of advertising, well, perhaps I am. But before you condemn all advertising professionals as liars, tricksters, hucksters, and charlatans, consider for a moment a stanza from a popular song: "If you took all the girls I knew when I was single / and brought them all together for one night / it could never match my sweet imagination / 'cause everything looks worse in black and white."

When the goal is to pierce through the tough, emotion-repellent fabric we call "intellect" so that we might speak more deeply to the needs of the heart, it appears to me that the great painters, sculptors, illustrators, and musicians point us toward the use of artistic exaggeration, "'cause everything looks worse in black and white." ❧

29

Poppin' the Rag

ONVERSATION HAD DWINDLED and we were riding in silence. Dad and I were rolling down the interstate, listening to the radio, when the music faded and the deejay began an energetic live ad for one of the advertisers. I'll always remember what Dad said when the announcer had finished his pitch: "That fella reminds me of a kid in New Orleans."

"Sorry, Dad, you lost me."

"I was walkin' down Bourbon Street early one morning when I stopped to watch a young boy shine a man's shoes. The customer was sittin' high up on this chair like a king on his throne and this kid was nothin' but a blur of sparks and elbows. He was really gettin' after it. Pop! Crack! Pow! went the shoeshine rag and I figured the man was going to walk off that stand with the shiniest shoes ever worn on human feet. So I waited around, expecting to see the first pair of wing-tips ever to be nominated to the Shoeshine Hall of Fame.

"Would you believe the shine was no big deal? The kid was just poppin' the rag. Now the guy on the radio who said all that happy stuff about that company . . . well, he was just poppin' the rag. He didn't tell me anything I hadn't heard a thousand times before, and he didn't give me any confidence that he was tellin' the truth or even believed what he was sayin'. He didn't give us any details or offer us any evidence. He was just poppin' the rag."

I want you to invest five minutes to help me prove a theory. Walk right now to the nearest radio and listen to the next commercial break. How often does an ad contain new information that leads you to a new conclusion? How often is the ad truly memorable, as opposed to merely clever? Are the writers of these ads persuasive, or merely creative? How often are they just "poppin' the rag"?

The next time you hear someone say, "I tried advertising, but it doesn't work for my kind of business," ask to see the ads he ran. Chances are he could learn a valuable lesson on Bourbon Street.

Effective advertising, like a deep shine on good leather, is a wonder to behold. But "poppin' the rag" is just "poppin' the rag." ❧

30

Intrusive Visibility

 LOCATION WITH INTRUSIVE VISIBILITY will cost you plenty to buy, rent, or lease, but it's usually the most efficient advertising your ad dollar can buy.

One of my favorite success stories revolves around the decision to move a forty-year-old store exactly one mile. The pivotal moment came when the client said, "I like the location, but it would cost eighty thousand a year, and my occupancy budget is only sixty thousand."

I told him, "Take the additional twenty thousand from the advertising budget. We can do more with a forty-thousand-dollar ad budget in that location than with a sixty-thousand-dollar ad budget somewhere else."

The land was purchased, the building built, and Opening Day was soon upon us. Having borrowed heavily, my anxious client phoned for some "advertising magic" to fill his new store with customers. I said, "Buy a banner four feet high and twenty feet long that says 'Now Open' on both sides. Place it perpendicular to the road so traffic can see it from both directions."

"Okay. What else?"

"That's it. That's all we're going to do. I don't believe you have the inventory or the staff to handle more of a crowd than the banner will bring you."

My client's sales volume during the first three months exceeded the previous twelve. The secret? Intrusive visibility. Tens of thousands of people had seen the store under construction, and every one of them was curious to see inside. Why? Intrusive visibility.

Don't confuse intrusive visibility with mere visibility or "traffic count." Intrusive visibility is the quality that sets landmarks apart from scenery.

How do you determine whether a location has intrusive visibility? Simple! Intrusive visibility means people see you when they're not looking for you. Intrusive visibility means the average person can immediately picture the building in his mind when you casually mention its location.

Intrusive visibility isn't always available, but when you can get it, it's worth whatever you have to pay.

31

A Fire Hose and a Teacup

 OU LIVE IN AN OVERCOMMUNICATED SOCIETY. The radio that awakens you gives you at most twelve minutes of music before you are forced to endure three minutes of commercials. Still half asleep, you roll out of bed to see your newspaper beckoning from your driveway even as your television clamors for your attention. You find advertising on your cereal box, coupons in your coffee, billboards alongside the road. You go to a restaurant for a relaxing meal only to be bombarded by messages in the windows, advertising on the place mats, and those evil little signs next to the salt and pepper shakers that tempt you with pictures of desserts you don't need. Then the waiter arrives to tell you about today's specials. In the words of a well-known comic-strip character, "Information is gushing toward your brain like a fire hose aimed at a teacup."

Is it any wonder people hate advertising? The noise of color and sound we endure each day can make us feel like we're living on the Midway surrounded by carnival barkers shouting for our attention. There's more to see and do than we can possibly accomplish.

Being intelligent creatures, we have developed complex defenses to guard us from this blight of color and sound. We've become immune to many phrases, statements, and tones of voice. Don't believe me? There are literally dozens of advertisers in your city who are spending gigantic sums to scream, "Highest quality at the lowest prices." Can you name them? On the other hand, there's one quiet, down-home fellow who drawls, "We'll leave the light on for ya." Can you tell me who he represents?

The public no longer pays attention to advertising that is obviously advertising, because it is, after all, "only advertising." The best (and the worst) ads today are a new breed I call Non Ads. The best Non Ads clearly communicate the benefit of a product in a style that does not seem like advertising. The worst get so carried away with style that they lose their message; they fascinate, but they say absolutely nothing. Non Ads can be very persuasive, but like anything powerful, they can also be dangerous when used improperly.

If your advertising tells your story the way one person speaks to another and without any of the clichés or unsubstantiated claims that muddle most ads, then you've probably created a good Non Ad. Your staff may tell you the ads "don't sound right" because they aren't "slick" like other ads. But isn't that exactly what you are trying to accomplish? ❧

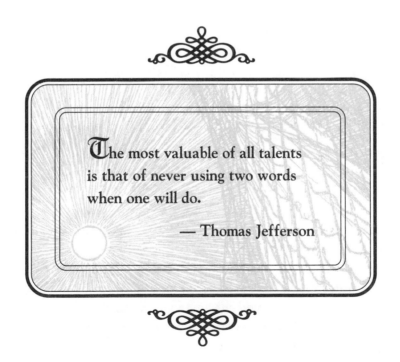

The most valuable of all talents is that of never using two words when one will do.

— Thomas Jefferson

32

A Few Magic Words

ISION, PASSION, FAITH, tenacity, perseverance, sacrifice. These things are part of a time-tested formula for success that's difficult to teach and painful to learn.

When the world sees a thriving business, the usual assumption is that the owner came up with a new angle or gimmick. To the casual observer, "he was lucky." Little is said or remembered about the man's failures, mistakes, or struggles; he was simply "lucky."

At our firm, the most difficult clients we serve are those who believe there's an angle or gimmick we can supply that will enable them to harvest easy money. When we ask these clients to tell us what makes their company different or special or better than their competitor's, their standard reply is "Nothing — that's what we pay you for."

The only real power we have as ad consultants is the ability to help the client tell his story as convincingly as possible. The assumption, of course, is that each client has a story to tell. To create a meaningful ad campaign, we must have the client's cooperation in helping us define his unique selling proposition. Too often, though, the client simply says, "Just bring more customers through our door. If you bring 'em in, we can sell 'em. What we need is more traffic."

Gee, what a great idea. Why didn't I think of that?

Good advertising would never be enough to save a restaurant known for lousy food, yet the chef would undoubtedly tell us, "Your job is to bring more customers through the door. If you bring them in, we can feed them."

If you see your business changing in ways you don't completely understand and you're ready to rethink the rules of your industry and press forward to a brighter tomorrow, what you need is an internal revolution and the ad campaign that results from it.

If you see your business changing in ways you don't completely understand and you simply want someone to walk into your world and say a few magic words and make everything better, you need a friend to pinch you, slap you, or shake you by the shoulders *because you're dreaming.* ❧

33

Albert's Big Observation

LBERT IS A WONDERFUL WRITER and an extreme introvert. Even though we've never met face to face, I still consider Al to be one of my best friends. Of all the things Albert has written, I am most intrigued by his observation that "we do things, but we do not know why we do them."

I've been there, Al. My study of advertising revolves around the question, "What makes people do the things they do?" Occasionally I catch a glimpse of understanding and create a compelling ad campaign from it, but for the most part, people remain a mystery to me. I don't know why we do what we do.

The poet Edwin Arlington Robinson was probably on the right track when he said, "The world is not a prison house, but a mass of millions of bewildered infants, all trying to spell GOD with the wrong blocks." Yet, when you take time to contemplate the matter, God is fairly easy to understand. He can be trusted unconditionally. It's people who are the tricky ones. This is why you should never fully believe what your customer tells you.

There's a profound difference between what a customer says she wants and what she truly wants. The diamond buyer says she wants a GIA certificate diamond of G color and VVS clarity when all she really wants is to see people's eyebrows jump to their foreheads as they exclaim, "Is that real?" The customer says she wants car wax when all she really wants is a shiny car. The business owner says she wants advertising when all she really wants is more customers.

People do things without fully understanding why they do them, and therefore they cannot be fully trusted when they tell you what they want. Will this little glimpse of insight cause you to reevaluate your sales pitch? It should.

Albert definitely hit the bull's-eye when he said, "We do things, but we do not know why we do them." Al has made hundreds of other fascinating little observations, but there is one in particular for which he is widely known.

One day Albert said, "E=mc²," and it literally rocked the world. ❧

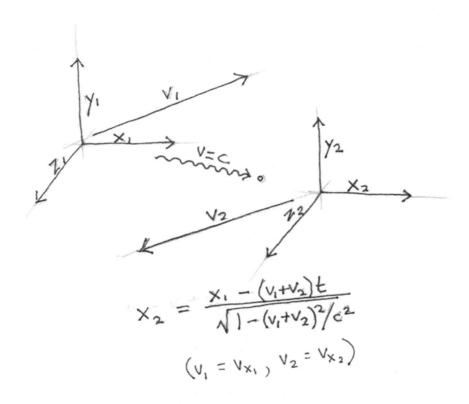

$$x_2 = \frac{x_1 - (v_1 + v_2)t}{\sqrt{1 - (v_1 + v_2)^2 / c^2}}$$

$$(v_1 = v_{x_1}, \quad v_2 = v_{x_2})$$

34

When You Need to Advertise in the Worst Possible Way

Step 1. Concentrate on reaching the "right people." There are plenty of "wrong people" out there who can't possibly do your business any good.

Step 2. Make sure you reach the largest number of "right people" you can possibly reach. It isn't important how often you reach them.

Step 3. Don't worry about what your ad says. The only thing that matters is whether your delivery is "smooth," "professional," and "classy."

Step 4. Fill your ad with the kinds of phrases and claims you've heard in other commercials. Your ad should sound like an ad!

Step 5. Discontinue any ad your friends don't like. Listen to what your neighbors say! Any ad that makes people uncomfortable can't possibly work.

Step 6. Let a TV or radio ad run just twenty to thirty times, then change it. Everyone has heard it and understands it by now.

Step 7. Don't be concerned about whether or not your delivery vehicle is intrusive. Passive advertising works just as well.

Step 8. Expect the public to have an intimate knowledge of your product. Use language unique to your industry.

Step 9. Impress the public. Prove your superior taste! The public is paying strict attention and doesn't miss a thing. Beautify the pages of the newspapers and magazines. People care more about your taste than about what your product will do for them.

Step 10. After completing steps one through nine, if you feel your advertising isn't working, what did you expect? These are the steps for advertising in the worst possible way! ≺∿

35

Twelve Causes
of Advertising Failure

1. The desire for instant gratification. The ad that creates enough urgency to cause people to respond immediately is the ad most likely to be forgotten immediately once the offer expires. Such ads are of little use in establishing the advertiser's identity in the mind of the consumer.

2. Trying to reach more people than the budget will allow. For a media mix to be effective, each element in the mix must have enough repetition to establish retention in the mind of the prospect. Too often, however, the result of a media mix is too many people reached without enough repetition. Will you reach 100 percent of the people and persuade them 10 percent of the way? Or will you reach 10 percent of the people and persuade them 100 percent of the way? The cost is the same.

3. Assuming the business owner knows best. The business owner is uniquely *un*qualified to see his company or product objectively. Too much product knowledge leads him to answer questions no one is asking. He's on the inside looking out, trying to describe himself to a person on the outside looking in. It's hard to read the label when you're inside the bottle.

4. Unsubstantiated claims. Advertisers often claim to have what the customer wants, such as "highest quality at the lowest price," but fail to offer any evidence. An unsubstantiated claim is nothing more than a cliché the prospect is tired of hearing. You must prove what you say in every ad. Do your ads give the prospect new information? Do they provide a new perspective? If not, prepare to be disappointed with the results.

5. Improper use of passive media. Nonintrusive media, such as newspapers and yellow pages, tend to reach only buyers who are actively looking for the product. They are poor at reaching prospects before their need arises, so they're not much use for planting a reticular activator or creating a predisposition toward your company. The patient, consistent use of intrusive media, such as radio and television, will win the heart of the customer before she's in the market for the product. Tell her Why; wait for When.

6. Creating ads instead of campaigns. It is foolish to believe a single ad can ever tell the entire story. The most effective, persuasive, and memorable ads are those most like a rhinoceros: they make a single point, powerfully. An advertiser with seventeen different things to say should commit to a campaign of at least seventeen different ads, repeating each ad enough to stick in the prospect's mind.

7. Obedience to unwritten rules. For some insane reason, advertisers want their ads to look and sound like ads. Why?

8. Late-week schedules. Advertisers justify their obsession with Thursday and Friday advertising by saying, "We need to reach the customer just before she goes shopping." Why do these advertisers choose to compete for the customer's attention each Thursday and Friday when they could have a nice, quiet chat all alone with her on Sunday, Monday, and Tuesday?

9. Overconfidence in qualitative targeting. Many advertisers and media professionals grossly overestimate the importance of audience quality. In reality, saying the wrong thing has killed far more ad campaigns than reaching the wrong people. It's amazing how many people become "the right people" when you're saying the right thing.

10. Event-driven marketing. A special event should be judged only by its ability to help you more clearly define your market position and substantiate your claims. If one percent of the people who hear your ad for a special event choose to come, you will be in desperate need of a traffic cop and a bus to shuttle people from distant parking lots. Yet your real investment will be in the 99 percent who did not come! What did your ad say to them?

11. Great production without great copy. Too many ads today are creative without being persuasive. Slick, clever, funny, creative, and different are poor substitutes for informative, believable, memorable, and persuasive.

12. Confusing reactions with results. The goal of advertising is to create a clear awareness of your company and its unique selling proposition. Unfortunately, most advertisers evaluate their ads by the comments they hear from the people around them. When we mistake mere response for results, we create attention-getting ads that say absolutely nothing. ❧

36

A Peek Behind the Curtain

O YOU REMEMBER THE SCENE in *The Wizard of Oz* in which Dorothy and her companions finally make it to the Emerald City, only to be refused entry to see the Great Oz? When they finally get inside, the four are greeted by fire, smoke, and a booming voice: "The Great Oz has spoken!" Just then, Toto, Dorothy's little dog, pulls back a curtain to reveal a rather ordinary-looking man pulling levers and shouting into a microphone. "Pay no attention to the man behind the curtain," booms the voice. "The Great Oz has spoken!"

Like most other celebrities, the "Great Oz" was mostly a myth created by a good ad man — the man behind the curtain.

Elvis Presley's agent, the reclusive and mysterious Colonel Parker, is paid exactly half of all the money Elvis makes, an amount that should ultimately total several million dollars. Most people think Colonel Parker was lucky to have discovered Elvis, but I strongly disagree. Elvis and I both know it was he who was lucky to have discovered the "Colonel."

Yes, I know Elvis agrees, because he continues faithfully to pay half his earnings to the Colonel, even though there has never been a written contract.

Like P. T. Barnum before him, Colonel Parker knows that the key to success is packaging.

The Colonel says, "Shut up and do what I tell you, boy, and we'll both get rich," and young Elvis listens. For every rhyming, dancing Cassius Clay you see in the boxing ring, you can be sure there's a Don King behind the curtain. Undiscovered talent is everywhere. I believe talent is probably the world's most abundant commodity. The hard thing to find is the man behind the curtain.

Anyone who says, "All I need is my talent," or "Determination is all it takes," or "Cream always rises to the top," will soon be bitterly disappointed. Which sells better, the best product, or the product with the best advertising?

There is an ancient proverb that says, "The race goeth not to the swift, nor the battle to the strong, but he who hath the best advertising leaveth them all in his dust." (Okay, so I changed the ancient proverb. Sue me.) ❧

Part Two

Turning Strangers
into Customers

37

The Best Salesman I Ever Knew

CHARLIE MYERS'S JOB WAS TO SELL USED CARS from a dumpy car lot on the wrong side of town. And sell them he did. Charlie knew nothing at all about cars, but he did know a lot about people.

The thing I remember best about Charlie was his upbeat attitude. Charlie was instantly and forever your friend — and there was nothing phony about it. Charlie believed that each day was going to be the best day of his life, and it often was.

The first time I saw him, he was dressed like a man going to the bank for a loan. I asked him what was the occasion. "No occasion," he replied. "I just believe that when you look right, you act right." Charlie didn't dress well to impress the customer; he dressed well because it gave him confidence. It made him feel in control. Charlie said it made him feel "ready."

One day when I had dropped in to visit Charlie, I noticed on his lot the most boring car I had ever seen. It was solid beige with no accent trim, and it even had a bench seat. I said, "Charlie, how in the world will you ever find a buyer for a car like that one?"

I'll never forget Charlie's answer. "Roy, there's a butt for every seat," he said. "That's Somebody's dream car, and I'm just waiting for Somebody to get here!"

Ultimately, Charlie Myers was discovered by a leading radio station and became "Cheerful Charlie," one of the most successful morning drive deejays of the decade. Tens of thousands of people enjoyed starting off their day to the sound of Charlie's voice.

The point I'm trying to make is this: Contrary to popular belief, selling isn't about having the right inventory. As Cheerful Charlie so eloquently phrased it, "There's a butt for every seat." Selling is simply "acting right."

In case you haven't yet figured it out, this story isn't just about my friend Cheerful Charlie, his opportunities, his inventory, or his customers. It's about you — your opportunities (they're all around you), your inventory (it's far more exciting than Charlie's), and your customers (they're ready to buy, and they're ready to buy *today*).

Now go sell something! ❧

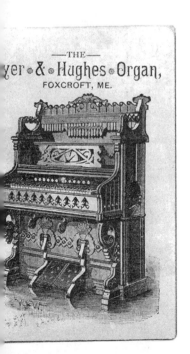

38

Cecil, Charlie, and Lagniappe

"I WAS CHARGED A FAIR PRICE" is not the statement of an excited customer, yet many business owners mistakenly believe they need only convince the public that they will be treated "fairly" to win their business. Phrases like "Honest Value for Your Dollar" and "Fair and Honest Prices" tempt me to say (with no small amount of sarcasm), "Yippee Skippy, call the press."

If the most your customer can say when he walks out your door is "I was treated fairly," your business is pitifully stale and you have virtually nothing to advertise. Why? Because the expectation of "fair treatment" is such a basic assumption in business dealings that most people take it for granted. What we really hope to find is the "delight factor."

Let's say Cecil owns a produce market and advertises that his scales are the most accurate in town. His competitor across the street, Fat Charlie, tends to be a little more expensive. Fat Charlie's produce is better, but the main reason people shop at Charlie's is the delight factor. Order ten pounds of potatoes and Charlie will happily toss potatoes onto the scale until it reads "10." Then, with a smile, he'll find a particularly nice potato, place it on the top of the pile, and exclaim, "Lagniappe!"

A Cajun word, "lagniappe" (LAN-yap) means "a little bit extra." If Fat Charlie doesn't add the extra potato, you can bet he'll hand you a juicy plum or a peach or a handful of fresh cherries from beneath the counter. But one thing is certain: Fat Charlie won't let you leave without lagniappe, the delight factor.

Cecil has chosen to be the town's low-cost provider and, as such, will always have a predictable customer base of bargain hunters. Fat Charlie, however, will enjoy more word-of-mouth advertising than Cecil and will also have a much higher average ticket due to the many add-on purchases he stimulates with his generous free samples.

Yet there is another, more subtle difference. As you walk out of Cecil's, you feel that you and he are "even." You got three dollar's worth of potatoes and Cecil got three dollars. Everyone who leaves Fat Charlie's, however, walks out with a feeling of delight. Charlie makes sure you get more than you anticipated. You never leave Fat Charlie's feeling "even."

Appealing to the emotions rather than the intellect, the delight factor is a powerful thing. If Cecil and Fat Charlie were in your town, where would you buy your produce? ❧

Life is like an echo.
We get from it what we put in it
and, just like an echo,
it often gives us much more.

— Boris Lauer-Leonardi

39

Idiots Are Out to Get Me

HE TELEPHONE RANG AND RANG. Thinking I must have dialed the wrong number, I was about to hang up when a voice answered and spoke the name of the store. "How late are you open tonight?" I asked. "We close at six o'clock sharp!" answered my anxious-to-leave young friend.

I had barely enough time to get there, but I really needed the item. I drove there as fast as I could.

As I walked through the door, the greeter looked at her watch with a frown, then glared at me. This much was clear: these people wanted to go home and I was keeping them from it. I was an unwelcome guest, and they wanted me gone.

I found what I needed as quickly as I could, not daring to look at any other merchandise. Digging cash out of my pocket, I hurried toward checkout.

Then I saw the line. Fourteen registers — only one of them open. You know the place, right?

While I waited in line, I watched as dozens of shoppers tried to enter the store, only to find the door locked. There might as well have been an employee standing out there shouting, "Go away, people, go away! You've got to leave the office early if you want to shop here!"

Finally it was my turn to give the cashier my money. "Thirty dollars and thirty-two cents, please," she said. Anxious to help her make change, I gave her three dimes, two pennies, and a fifty-dollar bill. "Fifty thirty-two," I said.

She stared at the fifty as if she had never seen one. Then she walked away to locate a manager.

Time passed. The people in line behind me grew restless. One sighed deeply, another muttered something that sounded like "sunny beaches." Finally, the cashier returned, dropped some money into my hand, and announced, "Nineteen sixty-eight."

Of course I pointed out her mistake, right? No, I didn't. Only one person in twenty-seven will say something in this situation, and I am one of the twenty-six.

I walked out to my car feeling sorry for whoever was in charge of advertising. When the sales volume of that store starts to slide, the ad manager will be called on the carpet and explanations will be demanded. This is when the ad manager should say, "This store pays lousy and hires idiots and doesn't train them, and people come here only as a last resort, because they're fed up with our incompetence."

But the truth would sound like blame shifting, so the ad manager will probably just hang his head, grind his toe into the carpet, and promise that he'll try to do better next time. ᙣ

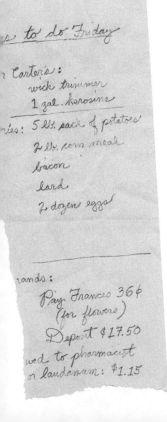

40

Does *Anyone* Lack Ambition?

WHEN PEOPLE WANT TO PAY a business person a compliment, they often say he "has a lot of ambition."

But ambition is as common as dirt. I've yet to meet a person who lacks it. I am therefore not convinced it is part of the great American formula for success.

I believe the vital ingredient is initiative.

Initiative means you take action. You work with what you've got. You never stand around waiting for instructions. You do something, even if it's wrong.

People who lack initiative hesitate to do what they cannot do well. Ambition without initiative is simply daydreaming.

An employee who has ambition without initiative spends his days trying to figure out what you can do for him. The employee with initiative is the one who tries to figure out what he can do for you. Both employees have ambition, but which do you think will rise higher? Make more money? Have more job offers?

Employees with initiative are needed, and they are needed badly. They are needed in every business in America. They are needed because they find solutions for the problems pointed out by the merely ambitious. They are the glue that holds a business together.

"Anything worth doing is worth doing well." That's what we've been taught. And yet — have you ever golfed or played tennis? Did you play well your first time out? No. But you went back and played badly a second time, because you understood that playing badly was part of the price of learning to play well.

A person with initiative says, "Anything worth doing is worth doing badly until I've learned to do it better. If it's worth doing, it's worth doing."

Always be quick to forgive the employee whose initiative causes you trouble. In the final analysis, this person is a gift from heaven.

𝕴 do the best I know how, the very best I can; and I mean to keep on doing it to the end. If the end brings me out all right, what is said against me will not amount to anything. If the end brings me out all wrong, ten angels swearing I was right would make no difference.

— Abraham Lincoln

41
A Breakfast Biscuit with Coffee

OY," SAID MY FRIEND CARL, "contrary to popular belief, the opposite of love isn't hate."

After a moment's consideration, I turned and looked at him quizzically.

Carl explained: "The opposite of love, my friend, is indifference."

I've decided Carl was right. Love and hate — powerful emotions both — are separated by only a thin line. We've all seen lovers become the bitterest of enemies, and we've watched once bitter rivals become the greatest of friends. Love and hate have much in common. The opposite of both is indifference.

There are many companies in America to which I am totally indifferent — companies that, to me, are "invisible." Perhaps the most invisible of all were Hardee's fast-food restaurants.

Hardee's invisibility began when I stopped at one in Missouri and witnessed a very uncomfortable moment at the sales counter. It could easily have happened anywhere, but it happened at Hardee's.

A few days later, at another Hardee's, the egg was cold on my breakfast biscuit. Doubtless they would have replaced it, but not wanting to complain, I just threw it away.

The following weekend, when Pennie suggested we pull into Hardee's, I objected. She told me I was being silly, and I probably was, but five minutes after we pulled away from the drive-thru window, Hardee's fate was sealed. My iced-tea cup had a tiny hole in the bottom. Before I knew what was happening, my crotch was soaked. Hardee's instantly became invisible.

I can honestly say that in the following eight years I never saw another Hardee's anywhere in America, until one day I found myself ravenously hungry in an unfamiliar part of Austin. The only eatery in sight was Hardee's. Reluctantly I pulled up to the drive-through microphone and ordered a breakfast biscuit with coffee.

"Would you like cream in your coffee, sir?" asked a pleasant voice.

"Sure, cream would be nice," I answered.

"One container or two?"

"I'd like two, please. Thanks for asking," I said — thinking, When did fast-food places start giving this kind of service?

"Would you like me to go ahead and stir the cream into the coffee for you, sir?" Wow! Hardee's not only became visible in my world, it became larger than life. With service like that, is it any wonder I decided the biscuit was the best I'd ever eaten?

A lady whose face I never saw renewed my confidence in Hardee's simply by offering to stir the cream into my coffee. Have you ever tried stirring cream into coffee while driving a car? Why has no one else ever offered to stir cream into my coffee?

Am I the only person in America who is this trivial, petty, and autocratic, or is there a chance the people who do business with your company might be as easily won — or lost?

The fate of your company is in the hands of your people. Train them well. ❧

42
Of Sharks and Pigs

T IS A TRUE BUT LITTLE-KNOWN FACT that more American citizens are killed by pigs each year than by sharks.

I believe this is also true of American businesses.

Business owners spend most of their time worrying about the sharks — those diabolical demon competitors — though it is far more likely to be the pigs who kill the company.

The pigs are the employees who would rather lie in the mud and oink than jump through hoops for a customer. The pigs are the middle managers who are more concerned with getting the most out of the company than with getting the most out of their staff. The pigs are the owners whose only thoughts are for short-term profits.

A healthy, pig-free company is one with a powerful sense of mission and purpose, a company with values that run deep enough to create a strong company culture. I've always known this to be true, but until now I've lacked the bona fide evidence to convince you.

In their most recent book, James Collins and Jerry Porras share some fascinating data from their research on corporate success. If a person had invested $1 in a group of "average" companies in 1926, his investment would be worth $415 today. Had he invested it in "good" companies, he would have $995. But when Collins and Porras focused their investigation on companies built on a core ideology — companies that refused to compromise their essential values, that remained true to their sense of mission even when it meant turning away from short-term profits — the hypothetical dollar paid back $6,356!

Bill Barclay owns eleven gas stations. Bill was a marine, and I'll bet he was a good one, because his staff of more than fifty gas station attendants is the most electric bunch of people you'll ever encounter. The services they perform are done exactly right and extraordinarily fast because these people love their work. With uniforms crisp and attitudes bright, Bill's employees fill the tank, check the oil, inflate the tires, and wash the windows with amazing speed. Bill Barclay never has the cheapest gasoline, but he always has the most customers. The marvelous profitability of Bill's company is merely the by-product of his passion for exceptional customer service and crisp corporate discipline. Sharks be damned.

Bill Barclay ignores the sharks and makes bacon of the pigs, and it seems to work pretty well for him. Maybe we should give it a try. ᴥ

43

"...which means..."

EATURES AND BENEFITS." Isn't this always Lesson One in any sales training program? Yet few of us ever master the art of translating the "feature" into a "benefit" our customer is prepared to buy!

"This car has a V-8 engine, you'll *love* it."

"The clarity grade of this diamond is SI-1. That's just above SI-2 and I-1 but below Flawless, VVs, and VS."

"We use a timed-release, granulated fertilizer instead of a liquid. It works much better."

"These bedsheets have 330 threads per inch, while most have only 180."

Obviously, these salespeople have assumed the customer has a level of understanding he simply does not have. (The salesperson often knows too much about his business and consequently assumes such information to be common knowledge.) Being on the inside looking out, the salesperson thinks, "Heck, everyone knows that!" But not everyone does. It's an easy trap to fall into, and the most knowledgeable salespeople are the most likely to do it.

How can we guard against making statements concerning features without benefit? A client shared a tip with me the other day that he said was making him a lot of money. B. J. has trained himself to silently add the words "which means" to the end of every statement he makes during a sales presentation. The result is that he is continually reminded to translate all the objective, intellectual features of his product into the meaningful, desirable benefits they represent: "This car has a V-8 engine, which means it will last longer because it doesn't have to work as hard as a smaller engine. You'll also have the power to pass in traffic, and most important, you'll have the acceleration to get out of the way of traffic accidents before they happen."

"The clarity grade of this diamond is SI-1, which means there are no visible inclusions to the naked eye, which means there is nothing whatsoever to detract from its amazing beauty, which means this diamond will appear flawless to anyone who sees it on her finger."

"We use a timed-release, granulated fertilizer, which means your lawn will be fed fertilizer in small amounts every day, which means your grass will stay green much longer than if we used liquid fertilizer."

"These sheets have 330 threads per inch, which means they will feel much softer on your skin and last much longer than normal sheets, which have only 180 threads per inch."

Learn to translate features into the language of the customer, whose only question is, "What's in it for me?" The customer will hear you when you speak his language. ꙮ

THE RUNABOUT

Black. All-steel body. Large compartment under rear deck. Weatherproof side curtains opening with both doors. Four cord tires, nickeled head lamp rims, windshield wiper. Starter and de-mountable rims $85 extra. Balloon tires $25 extra. Price f. o. b. Detroit.

$260

44

Three, Four, and Three

O MATTER WHAT SELLING STYLE a salesperson may use, the odds are he'll instantly hit it off with three out of ten people. Four out of ten will be able to take him or leave him, and the final three aren't going to like him no matter what he says. Most salespeople make their living selling the three out of ten with whom they find an easy connection; the sales champion learns how to handle the four in the middle.

The sales champion has learned to recognize and adapt to the basic temperament of the person he is selling. Here's what I mean by "basic temperament." Four people (we'll call them Pencil, Rhino, Hugger, and Wally) hear the same sales presentation and have the following reactions.

Pencil: "I thought it was very informative. He knew his information."

Rhino: "I was bored out of my wits. Ask that guy for the time of day and he'll tell you how to build a clock."

Hugger: "I liked him. He seemed sincere."

Wally: "Let me show you how I would have done it."

The same four now listen to a presentation from a second salesperson:

Pencil: "The presentation was thin and he rushed through it."

Rhino: "I think he made a lot of sense! He made his point and shut up!"

Hugger: "He seemed a little high strung; maybe he's having a bad day."

Wally: "He had more pizzazz than the first guy, but I could still do it better."

Can you imagine four such different people? Sure you can! You already know people just like these guys, right? Since the time of the ancient Greek Hippocrates, it has been known that each of the millions of different personalities in our human race will fall into one of four basic temperament groups. Pencil is of the Analytical temperament, Rhino is a Driver, Hugger is known as an Amiable, and Wally is an Expressive.

Your goal as a salesperson is to learn to identify each of the four temperaments and to alter your sales pitch to fit the preference of the prospect — to give each of them what he wants.

The Analytical (Pencil) wants accuracy: "Just the facts, please."

The Driver (Rhino) wants accomplishment: "Let's get this thing done!"

The Amiable (Hugger) wants acceptance: "Can't we all be friends?"

The Expressive (Wally) wants applause: "Pay attention to me."

Personality typing will never be an exact science. However, it can be a valuable tool for helping us see through the eyes of others. ❧

The Platinum Rule:
Do unto others as they prefer to be done unto.

— Otto Kroeger

45

Flash! Commoners Outnumber the Rich

THINK OF ALL THE TRULY WEALTHY PEOPLE you've met. How many of them became wealthy by catering to the needs of the rich?

It should take you only a moment to realize that very few wealthy people made their money by selling to rich people. Most of the rich made their millions by doing something incredibly basic. Elemental. Fundamental. Simple.

Learn the story of the people who live in the house on the hill, and you'll probably learn they own the rural garbage service in twelve counties: "We made our money with trash trucks." Or their great-grandfather invented tubeless tires. Or they make boxes.

The amount of money you make will be determined by the size of problem you solve.

There are two ways a problem can be considered "big." A problem can be big because it threatens the peace of mind of a single individual. Heart surgeons are paid for solving this type of big problem.

Another way a problem can be big is if it's shared by virtually everyone. "How can I bundle these papers together without stapling them?" Any idea how many paper clips are sold each year?

People who make a living by serving the rich are called "butlers." ❧

The man who sells to the classes will live with the masses. Sell to the masses and you'll live with the classes.

46

Yes, I'm Prejudiced. So Sue Me

AM SMALL ENOUGH to have absurd little prejudices, but I am also big enough to admit it. Oddly, though, I have none of the traditional stupid prejudices we typically associate with the word. I have my own brand of stupid prejudices.

One of the most longstanding of these prejudices has been against men with ponytails. I've always felt that guys with ponytails were painfully complacent. They never seemed to be bad people, they just lacked the enthusiasm to be good at anything. A ponytail was the unmistakable sign of yaaaawning apathy. A man with a ponytail was a tragic waste of skin.

My ponytail prejudice was recently ground into dust and blown into the night breeze on the island of Kona, Hawaii. Pennie, the boys, and I were having dinner at a popular restaurant. You couldn't have wedged another person into that place with a shoehorn, and there were dozens more waiting impatiently outside. It was a scene beyond frantic; this place was a madhouse. We were seated and told "Sam" would be our waiter.

I judged Sam in a glance. You guessed it. Down to his waist.

But Sam Hori rocked my world that night, and it began the moment he introduced himself. We didn't get the obligatory plastic-coated greeting. Sam was friendly and relaxed; he made my family feel comfortable in an environment where I would never have thought it possible. My interest deepened when Sam offered his appetizer recommendations. He seemed somehow more sincere than the typical waiter, so I ordered both of the appetizers he recommended, along with two of my own choosing. Sam's favorites were clearly the winners. Mine were good; his were fabulous.

But I couldn't get past the ponytail. I said to myself, "He has a strong opening, but I'll bet he fades in the finish." I had barely completed the thought when Sam arrived to refill our glasses, clear the appetizer dishes, and bring us more bread.

I decided Sam must have only two or three tables to wait. This would explain the lavish service. So I began watching. I soon realized that Sam was responsible for several tables, and that each of them was getting the same charming treatment my family was getting.

Then I decided, "It must come to him naturally." But as I continued to watch, I realized that when Sam was not tableside, he was a veritable blur of efficiency. This wasn't just natural talent — Sam Hori was working his butt off.

"I've got it! Sam is an expensive consultant the owner imported from the mainland to train his other waiters!" When he returned, I casually asked, "Sam, where are you from, originally?" Sam smiled his amazing smile and told us he had been born and raised on Kona and was thrilled to have found a job so close to home.

That did it. I knew I would write about Sam. But as they say, talk is cheap. So I added 20 percent to the tab I was paying by credit card and then looked Sam in the eye. "Sam," I said, "my business has taken me into thirty-eight states and three foreign countries, and I've eaten at no less than one thousand of the finest restaurants in the world. I tell you this only so you will grasp my meaning when I say that you are the best waiter I have ever seen." And with that I pressed into his hand a one-hundred-dollar bill. I would have felt guilty had I done less.

What does any of this have to do with you? It's simple. Sam Hori walked into a situation where the deck was stacked against him, and he won. He had no chance, but he won. He had every excuse to "fail with honor," but he won. The place was crowded, people were waiting, and some idiot customer was prejudiced against his haircut, but he won. Have you ever had the deck stacked against you? Have you ever been dealt a raw deal? Have you ever felt that you had no chance? Have you ever had an idiot customer?

Sam Hori waits tables, and in my opinion, he is the best waiter on earth. Who is the best at what you do? ♋

Do what you know best; if you're a runner, run, if you're a bell, ring.

— Ignas Bernstein

47

A Caterpillar Named John Riley

OHN RILEY IS AVERAGE in every way but one. When speaking of sports, or cars, or fishing, or business, or travel, John Riley is painfully, excruciatingly average. But let the discussion turn to wine, and this caterpillar named John Riley becomes a monarch butterfly before your eyes.

The butterfly dance begins as Riley darts from shelf to shelf, snatching bottles and babbling phrases you don't completely understand. His harvest complete, Riley opens each bottle with the delicate precision of a neurosurgeon and slowly pours for each of the people watching.

As the wine trickles into the glasses, Riley's eyes sparkle as he describes what you are about to taste. "This Ravenswood single-vineyard Zinfandel is as reckless and uninhibited as a New Orleans Mardi Gras." Sipping the wine, you taste uninhibited reckless-ness and, as surely as the sun rises in the east, hear faint echoes of jazz. Now, using his hands, John illustrates how the next wine is "dripping with fruit. A rain shower of fruit has been captured in this very bottle." As you taste the wine, the sensation of fruit is like nothing you've ever experienced. John Riley's show is defi-nitely worth the price of admission.

My favorite Riley moment came when John gathered a faraway look in his eyes and the room grew silent. He looked at each of us, one at a time, then shook his head slowly from side to side as he stretched his hand gently toward a dusty bottle. I thought of Captain Ahab and Moby Dick as John Riley whispered in a voice thick with reverent awe, "The Philip Togni cabernet is a dark . . . brooding . . . monster."

It was never my intention to acquire an expensive collection of wine. I just wanted to buy a few bottles for celebratory toasts at the office. My problem is that I met John Riley. But I'm convinced Riley's ability to sell wine has nothing to do with technique; I doubt that he ever attended a sales seminar or even once sat through a training class. Riley's ability to sell wine was born of passion. Raw passion for his product, unconditional humility, and impressive product knowledge are what make John Riley's wine recommendations irresistible.

I've known other men with similar passions, and each of them is wildly successful. When Woody Justice describes a diamond, or Joe Romano speaks of activity-based accounting, or Jon Silva describes the wonders of the deep, or Tom Pelton talks about Jesus, you don't have a chance. The passion of these men makes their offer irresistible.

Their offer to you is this advice: "Love what you do; the money will follow." ❧

ard's Almanack

brethren of the commonwealth of Pennſylvania ...unto the maſſes the benefits for themſelves and ...atever suffice to enſure one's continued exiſtence.

A man in a paſſion rides a wilde horſe.
-- B. Franklin

TO ALL CITIZENS

48

Abraham Lincoln!

HE NAME "ABRAHAM LINCOLN" conjures a lot of powerful images, doesn't it? Ask ten people what Abe Lincoln means to them, and you're likely to get as many different answers. "Freed the slaves." "Kept the nation together." "Stuck by Grant when Grant was criticized." "Taught himself to read and write with a piece of charcoal on the back of a shovel in a log cabin."

These are the answers you would expect, things you already knew. But the part of Honest Abe I like best is the part not often mentioned in the history books — something he said:

"Things may come to those who wait, but only the things left by those who hustle."

Yes, that's right. Abe was a hustler, a fighter, a scrapper, an opportunist. How else does a dirt-poor farm boy become president of the United States? Abraham Lincoln knew that opportunity is everywhere, and that "all men are created equal."

In Lincoln's eyes, the factors that set men apart were attitude and effort. Using these things as a measuring stick, Abe would be the first to agree that some men have made themselves "more equal" than others.

The average salesperson in America will close two out of ten selling opportunities; he'll tell you, "Selling is a numbers game. If you want me to sell more, bring me more selling opportunities." But an excited, motivated, informed, "I love my job" salesperson will close half of all the people he sees each day, generating nearly three times the dollars produced by the "average" salesperson.

I think Abe would have sold 100% and then bought your store

Do you realize that all the people you will see today are hoping to buy something from you?

Please don't disappoint them.

49
Management by Consensus

 HAVE SO OFTEN BEEN TOLD "it's lonely at the top" that I've concluded it must be loneliness that causes business owners to succumb to the degenerative, debilitating business disease known as "management by consensus." Symptoms include apathy, confusion, a lack of focus and direction, loss of the ability to wholeheartedly commit, and finally, financial decline. The most devastating effect of management by consensus, however, is analysis paralysis. "Since we can't agree on a solution, we'll just study the problem some more."

Please don't confuse the popular concept of employee empowerment with management by consensus. Employee empowerment means you give your employees the authority to do their jobs; management by consensus means you give your employees the authority to do *your* job.

Business owners who are guilty of managing by consensus will usually agree that "a camel is a racehorse designed by a committee," because very few of them ever realize that managing by committee is exactly what they are doing. "What? I'm not managing by committee! I always make the final decision! I just like to keep my team leaders involved."

Abraham Lincoln was a gifted, visionary leader who also liked to "keep his team leaders involved." Abe's team leaders were his presidential cabinet, and he always sought their input before making an important decision. On one historic occasion when a vital measure was in debate, the cabinet members were unanimous in their recommendation against it. Lincoln listened intently, thanked each of them sincerely for their help, and closed by saying, "I, however, vote yes. The measure passes."

Lincoln sought the input of his team leaders, not their approval.

Leadership is not a matter of genius. It's a matter of courage. I believe those business owners who manage by consensus do so because they want to share the responsibility for failure. Consensus lets them escape the haunting possibility they may someday have to look in the mirror and say, "I, alone, was wrong." ❧

50

Time Poverty

 IME IS THE CURRENCY OF OUR GENERATION. The supply is limited, and everyone needs more of it. Time has become the great equalizer. Each of us is given an identical twenty-four hours each day, and our success is largely determined by how we use these hours.

A recent survey of American business owners revealed near-unanimous agreement on the most important factors in considering an employee for advancement. Topping the list was the employee's ability to separate the important from the trivial — to prioritize. Employers don't want their people wasting time on that which is not important.

The second most highly valued characteristic was the ability to get things done speedily. In summary: the most highly valued employees are those who can quickly decide what to do and then get it done. It's all about saving time.

Never in the history of the world has a nation had so many appliances and services devoted to the saving of time, and never has a nation had so little free time. The growing trend toward time poverty explains why most Americans will decide whether they have any interest in a thing within seven seconds of their first exposure to it. This incredibly short attention span makes it nothing less than vital that your salespeople train themselves to get to the point.

This trend is so self-evident that I fear we often overlook it. Remember the advice J. Paul Getty gave when asked how to become rich? "Find a need and fill it." The need of today's customer is to save time. How many ways do you offer to save your customers time?

Getting people's money is easy once you have persuaded them to give you their time. Win the time of the people and their money will follow. ❧

Do you love life?
Then do not squander time,
For that's the stuff life is made of.

— Benjamin Franklin

51

When an Idea's Time Has Come

UST AS ALBERT HAS HIS THEORY OF RELATIVITY, I have my own Theory of Universal Knowledge, which states, "There is a time for every idea, and when that time comes, the idea springs into the minds of several people simultaneously."

It is the first person to take action who gets all the applause; the rest just sit back and cry, "He stole my idea!" Though the world is overflowing with good ideas, people with the courage to act are rare.

Swann and Sawyer are brilliant inventors working on opposite sides of the Atlantic. Each of them has plans to produce electric light by running a current through a filament in a vacuum. But it is Thomas Edison who first announces the discovery and receives all the fame and fortune. It doesn't matter that both Swann and Sawyer are further advanced in their experiments, or that it will be more than a year before Edison publicly produces electric light. Edison has the courage to claim he can do it. Sawyer and Swann do not.

Instances of universal knowledge are becoming increasingly commonplace due to the rapid growth of our population and the influence of mass communication. With millions and millions of people receiving identical information and stimuli, should it come as any surprise that many of us have the same ideas at about the same time?

Evidence of genius is becoming commonplace and talent seems to be running rampant in our world. I'll wager that you, yourself, have enough talent to be world famous for something! The important question is this: Are you willing to take action, or will your talent remain unrefined, like gold that stays in the ground?

Are we, in fact, created in the image of God? And if so, does this mean that each of us is a walking miniature of Him who spoke worlds into existence and flung the stars from His fingertips? Did He, in fact, prepare you to do great things, then give you the choice as to whether you would do them? Is there a chance that your circumstances and experiences have uniquely and wonderfully prepared you for such a time as this?

Do you have the courage to act? ∽

52

When the Time Has (Not Yet) Come

 HEN WE SAY, "HE WAS THE FIRST," we are usually talking about a person whose idea succeeded brilliantly. When we say, "He was ahead of his time," we are typically speaking of someone who was equally brilliant, but whose idea failed miserably. Both were ahead of their time; the second was simply too far ahead.

I've explained my theory regarding the likelihood of universal knowledge when an idea's time has come. I've encouraged you to put your ideas into action quickly, rather than let someone else beat you to the punch. Now, however, I feel I must warn you of the pitfalls of being too quick to take action. A great many business disasters have been caused by visionary people who took action a little too soon.

The pivotal question is this: Has the time for your idea truly come, or are you a visionary too far ahead of your time?

Thomas J. Watson owns a company that makes mechanical adding machines. When Watson hears of a new device called a "computer," he takes the time to investigate. Watson concludes, "I think there is a world market for about five computers," and allows Sperry-Rand to beat him to the punch. Sperry-Rand's computer, the Univac, fails miserably. It is an idea ahead of its time.

Thomas J. Watson's company, International Business Machines, continues to prosper until the time for computers arrives. Now Watson's people leap into action, waiting for nothing. Their efforts quickly launch IBM into the lead as the most powerful computer company in the world.

Has the time come for your idea? Should you rush headlong

into action, or would it be wiser to hide and watch the pioneers get shot full of arrows? Unfortunately, there's no way to be sure. The question to be answered is this: When you envision the success of your idea, is that success based on the way things ought to be or on the way things really are?

The ideas that fail are usually the ones promoted by people who refuse to accept reality. Are you counting on things being as they ought to be, or are you accepting circumstances as they really are? Answer this question, and you will know whether the time for your idea has truly come. ∽

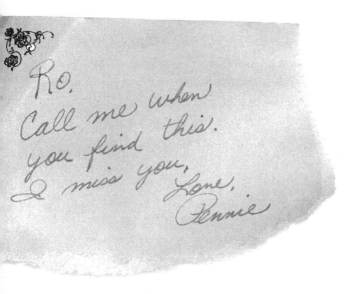

Ro,
Call me when
you find this.
I miss you,
Love,
Pennie

53

Five Happy, Nine Disappointed

THE STORE HAD EXACTLY TEN CUSTOMERS being served by exactly ten salespeople when I walked in. I was odd man out for quite a while, so I spent my time looking in case after case, anxiously waiting for someone to offer help.

After a while I began to work at looking conspicuous. I would stand in front of a showcase, stare intently at an item I wanted to buy, then look around hoping to catch someone's eye. No luck. I walked to another case and tried the same thing. Not a nibble.

As I left the store, I thought, "Maybe I'll come back another day when they're not so busy." But in my heart I knew I would never return. Lots of places make me feel good when I visit. Why should I go back to one that doesn't? Although I can't say I had a bad experience, I definitely left disappointed.

I have no idea whether the owner of that store even knew I was there. I was greeted by no one. But if the owner saw me as I walked out, he probably assumed I wasn't ready to buy or that I didn't see anything I liked.

If this had happened in your store, would you have known it?

I've got a friend by the name of Brad Huisken who's a crackerjack sales trainer. Brad tells me of a recent nationwide survey that says 67 percent of all shoppers intend to return home with the item they are shopping for, but that only 24 percent actually do so.

How many people leave your store disappointed each day? This survey tells us that for every five sales you make, another nine customers who had hoped to buy from you will leave your store disappointed and empty-handed. This means your existing store traffic can give you 2.8 times your current sales volume, if you sell only those customers who are ready to buy!

Any investment in sales training is an investment in your own gross profits. The only thing more expensive than hiring a sales trainer is *not* hiring one. ❧

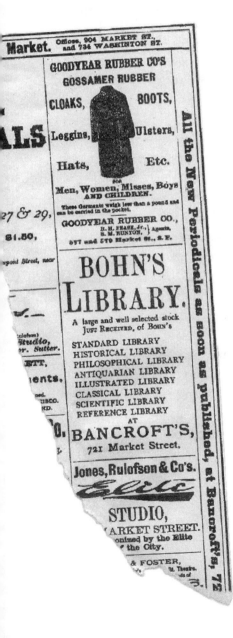

54

A Merry-Go-Round Called Kansas

DOROTHY THINKS OF KANSAS as a merry-go-round where she lives her life to the tedious rhythm of a cosmic calliope. Apart from the noise and the ups and downs, Dorothy feels she's just going around in circles. She isn't entirely happy in Kansas.

How do you feel about Kansas?

Kansas is the place where you know your way around — where there are few hidden dangers and every day is the same. But is Kansas really so bad? Mundane, yes. Predictable, yes. Boring? Certainly. But it's safe.

Do you feel your life has too much safety? Do you feel stuck on a merry-go-round? Is every day the same? No, there's adventure to be had in Kansas, but are you sure you want an adventure?

Adventures come with trouble. It's part of the package. Remember Dorothy and Toto in Oz? It didn't take long before Dorothy was clenching her eyes and saying, "There's no place like home. There's no place like home."

Are you really sure you want an adventure? Are you ready to leave behind all that's familiar? Are you ready to make weird alliances and fight unimagined evils? Not everyone is ready for a trip to Oz, though it's not a hard place to find.

You've just got to be willing to ride a tornado.

Are you willing? ❧

Nothing stirs up a whirlwind of controversy quite so quickly as radical advertising

55

Falling off the Merry-Go-Round

HEN THE MERRY-GO-ROUND was a new thing, Americans thought going around in circles was fun. The novelty, however, soon wore off and the business faded. Then a clever merry-go-round operator hung a brass ring on a hook, just beyond the reach of his riders. Responding instinctively to the challenge, they began to lean off their horses each time they saw the brass ring come into view. Many of them fell on their heads.

The riders leaned and stretched and reached because it was the instinctive thing to do, even though the best way to gain the brass ring would obviously have been to hop off the horse, walk over to the hook, and grab it.

Business is like that. Most business people never consider approaching a problem directly. They prefer to study how to become better at leaning. They want to bring about change without really changing.

Do you want to solve your problem? Get off your high horse and plant your feet on the ground. ᑫᔕ

56

Perception of Value

ALUE." NOW, THERE'S A WORD that defies explanation. My little dictionary gives a fuzzy definition, then offers several examples of the word in use, such as "What is its market value?" "Sold it below its value." "Got good value for his money."

What is value? If your goal as a merchant is to deliver good value, you must first have an understanding of how value is measured and what constitutes good and poor value in the eyes of the customer, right?

How, exactly, is value perceived and measured? Having pondered this question for a few decades, I think I'm finally ready to attempt a definition: Value, in the eyes of the customer, is simply the difference between the anticipated price and the marked price.

If the price anticipated in the customer's mind is higher than the price marked on the item, the customer perceives it to be a good value: "I would have thought it more expensive!" Yet if the asking price is higher than the anticipated price, the customer perceives the value to be poor: "This is highway robbery!"

The secret, then, is to control the anticipated price.

In the past, the merchant's control of the anticipated price was accomplished by simply "marking it up to mark it down." In essence, if the goal was to sell an item for $20, he would first mark it $40, then label it "Half Off." Today's customer is not so easily duped.

Elevation of the anticipated price is readily accomplished by product reputation, product presentation, interior lighting, and store decor. People expect things to cost more in prettier stores.

When they cost less than anticipated, the public perceives them to be a good value.

We expect food eaten by soft candlelight to cost more than food under harsh electric light. We expect a meal served by a waiter to cost more than the same meal in a cafeteria. But the cost of ingredients is the same at both restaurants. The difference in our perception of value is caused by reputation, presentation, lighting, and decor.

Advertising can help build your reputation, but don't expect your ads to change your presentation, lighting, and decor. You've got to do that on your own. 🙞

Restaurant Antoine
Fondé En 1840

AVIS AU PUBLIC
Faire de la bonne cuisine demande un certain temps. Si on vous fait attendre, c'est pour mieux vous servir, et vous plaire.

ENTRÉES (SUITE)

Ris de veau à la financière 4.00

Foie de volaille en brochette 3.00

Tripes à la mode de Caen (commander d'avance) 3.50

Noisette d'agneau Hawaïenne 5.00

Tenderloin tips en brochette béarnaise 4.00

Filet de boeuf nature 5.50

Côtelettes d'agneau grillées 4.25

Entrecôte nature 6.50

Tournedos nature 4.50

Châteaubriand (30 minutes—serves two) 15.00

Entrecôte minute 5.75

Filet de boeuf Robespierre en casserole (30 minutes) 6.75

SAUCES

Béarnaise .90   Médicis .90   Maison d'Or 1.10

Financière 1.10   à la Rossini 2.10

.90   Demi Bordelaise .90

.90

57

A Lateral Transfer of Knowledge

HEN A BUSINESS OWNER comes up with a new way to look at his business and it makes him a millionaire, you can be sure of one thing: the new idea isn't really new at all. The business owner has simply borrowed an already proven concept from a parallel but unrelated industry.

As Henry walks through a meat-packing house in Chicago, he sees that each of the butchers has a single, specialized function. Dividing a complex and tedious process into a series of specialized tasks is nothing new in the meat-packing business, but it is a revolutionary concept to Henry. He transfers the idea from meat packing to automaking, and it makes him one of the richest men in the world.

Hundreds of automakers were building cars long before Henry Ford built his first, but none of them ever saw a connection with meat packing. For more than thirty years, these automakers built cars one at a time and never looked for a better way, because "this is how everyone does it."

Henry Ford had the audacity to look at the auto industry and say, "Maybe everyone is wrong." Einstein looked at time and space and said, "Maybe everyone is wrong." Louis Pasteur looked at disease and said, "Maybe everyone is wrong." Columbus looked at the horizon and said, "Maybe everyone is wrong." Galileo looked at the stars and said, "Maybe everyone is wrong." Yet not one of these men began with a blank sheet of paper. Each of them was intrigued, inspired, and guided by the observations of others. Isaac Newton may have spoken for them all when he said, "If I have seen further than other men, it is because I have stood on the shoulders of giants."

Are you a good listener? Are you a thoughtful observer? Do you have respect for the fundamental worth of everything you see? Do you have the humility to accept that you may be wrong? It is an audacious humility indeed that says, "Perhaps we have been wrong all along."

Henry Ford was a miserable father and an arrogant tyrant, but somewhere beneath this brittle exterior, Henry possessed the humility to believe he could learn valuable things from a meat cutter.

It was this humility that made Henry his fortune. ❧

Everyone has something valuable he can teach you, schoolboy, if you'll only take the time to learn.

— Earl ("Ted") Tedder, steelworker, Broken Arrow, Oklahoma

58

Intellect and Emotion

 OES THE CUSTOMER TYPICALLY BUY the best value, or does she buy what she *feels* to be the best value? In reality, people usually do what their emotions dictate, then find the logic to justify it. Nothing is quite so important as emotion in advertising and selling. Regardless of what you sell, the important things to grasp are the intangibles.

As an expert in your industry, you see your product far more intellectually than does your customer. The benefits you see in your product are different from the benefits your customer sees. You see things that make your product different from your competitor's. Your customer sees only what your product will do for her — and chances are your competitor's product will do the same thing.

Your customer will buy whichever product she *feels* best about. Make sure she feels best about yours.

Advertising may increase the customer's emotional predisposition toward your store, as well as increase the number of selling opportunities you may have, but it often takes a salesperson to close the sale. Good advertising begins the process of selling, but it is a process that must be completed on the sales floor.

Do your salespeople know what your ads say? Are they in step with the spirit and thrust of the message you're sending the public? Listening to your salespeople should be like hearing an extension of your ads. If your advertising and your salespeople aren't saying the same thing, you must bring the two together.

The most effective selling organization will be the one whose external sales message (advertising) is in perfect harmony with its internal sales message (sales presentations). If your ad writers are marching to the beat of the same drum heard by your sales staff, there will be synchronicity and success. If they're marching to different rhythms or in different directions, there will be chaos.

How well do you play the drum? 𝄡

Intangibles are the most honest merchandise anyone can sell. They are always worth whatever you are willing to pay for them and they never wear out. You can take them to your grave untarnished.

— Lazarus Long

59

Silver Paint and a Weed-Eater

 HAVE A FRIEND NAMED TONY who gave his entire fortune to an oil lease speculator in return for mineral rights on 4,200 acres with a dozen oil wells. Even though oil speculators are notoriously ruthless, it never occurred to Tony that he might be putting his money at risk or that it might be helpful to have a basic understanding of the oil business. Tony isn't like the rest of us.

Two weeks after Tony paid for the oil lease, the price of oil began a sharp decline. Due to the unexpected costs of maintaining the oilfield equipment, Tony was soon down to his last few hundred dollars. The government then notified Tony that he could pump no more oil until he drilled an extremely expensive injection well to dispose of unwanted salt water. On paper, the oil lease was now unsalable. A quick glance at production records would make it obvious to any oil man that this particular oil field was a very risky investment.

"Tony, what are you going to do?" I asked.

"Wait and see," he answered.

Using a mower, a weed-eater, and several gallons of silver paint, Tony turned his 4,200 acres into such a beautiful park that I found myself looking for the flags on the putting greens. Sparkling silver pump jacks floated on a sea of immaculate green grass. I've seen state parks less beautiful. The oil business has always been the world's grimiest, yet here was a place you could bring the family for a picnic.

Even the most jaded, analytical, cold-blooded oil men were impressed with Tony's little wonderland. Men who had made fortunes by taking advantage of desperate and inexperienced investors were now bidding against each other to own Tony's oil park. Having already decided in his heart to buy the oil field, each man now studied the production records to see what might be done to increase oil recovery.

Silver paint and a weed-eater enabled Tony to recoup his initial investment, recover all his expenses, and make an additional $70,000. As for me, I learned a priceless lesson about the power of a compelling presentation.

My friend Tony knew oil men are like the rest of us: they find the intellectual logic to justify what their emotions have already decided. Using a weed-eater to create a powerful presentation, Tony recovered his fortune and with his profits bought a fleet of sports cars.

Is there a way to put the power of presentation to work in your business? ◞◟

60

The Way Things Ought to Be

WE HAVE A CLIENT I call "the Sanctimonious Bastard" — but it's okay, because I call him that only to his face, never behind his back.

"Sanc" lives in the Land of the Way Things Ought to Be, where he is an energetic crusader writing highly intellectual, multipage discourses concerning everything wrong with the world and what needs to be done about it.

In the Land of the Way Things Ought to Be, "Sanc" wears a bright red cape and tall black boots and has a big red "S" on the front of his costume. Unfortunately, in the Land of the Way Things Really Are, "Sanc" is just a regular guy with glasses and a Subaru.

Yet the world needs sanctimonious bastards. Without them, we would have no letters to the editor in our newspapers and magazines. We would never have the chance to sign all those worthwhile petitions, and no one would ever urge us to "Vote for Guidomeyer!" Without sanctimonious bastards there would be no social reform of any kind, and there might never have been a Boston Tea Party or an American Revolution. "Taxation without representation? Sounds okay with us, King George."

There's nothing wrong with being a sanctimonious bastard, but I need to warn you — there's no money in it, because most of the world lives in the Land of the Way Things Really Are, where the number-one song is "What's in It for Me?"

All of us have a little self-righteous sanctimony in us, but it's rarely good to include it in your advertising, and even more rarely does it profit you to carry it onto the sales floor. Pious experts do a very poor job of making people feel good.

Presidential candidate Walter Mondale was acutely aware of all that was wrong with America, and he offered clear advice about what we must do to become once again "a great and mighty, good and wonderful nation." On the other hand, we had a bright-eyed, cheerful Ronald Reagan assuring us that we were already "Great and Mighty, Good and Wonderful" and that we didn't need to do anything except try to have a good time.

History records who made the sale. Reagan won by one of the largest margins in the history of our nation.

Mondale may have had a better understanding of the problem, but Reagan understood the solution, which was simply this: Make people feel good. It's amazing what people can do when they feel good.

Can you make people feel good? More importantly, will you? ❧

61

A Two-Peso Weather Report

 RED PITEZEL IS A PILOT flying into Mexico with an uneasy feeling about the weather. Fred radios ahead for a weather report, knowing he must pay for all control tower services immediately upon landing. "Señor," asks a voice, "do you want the two-peso weather report — or do you want the fiiiiive-peso weather report?" Fred silently wonders how much the accuracy of the weather report changes with the price. "I think I'd prefer a ten-peso report if you've got one," he says. Fred Pitezel is a very wise man.

I am standing in the front yard of my close friend Loren Lewis when a blue Cadillac pulls into his driveway. Loren is known as a brilliant pool player, a wonderful storyteller, and a mechanical genius who has a weird, psychic bond with Cadillacs. Loren shouts to the driver, "Pop the hood and leave it running!" and then begins messing with things in the engine compartment before the man has even gotten out of his car.

While Loren is twisting bolts and pulling wires, the driver introduces himself and begins telling his sad story over Loren's shoulder. "I've had it every place in town and you're my last hope. This car has been in and out of the shop for the past two months, and I've spent more than five hundred dollars to fix the air conditioner, but it still won't blow cold. No one can figure it out. One of the guys at the dealership suggested I bring it to you, but I don't want to leave it here unless you're certain you can fix it."

Just then, Loren closes the hood and says, "I heard the problem as you were pulling into the drive. Now reach through the window and stick your hand in front of the vent."

The man's eyes widen. He shouts, "It's ice cold! It's ice cold!"

"That'll be fifty dollars," says Loren.

"What?" exclaims the man. "I've only been here three minutes. You can't charge me fifty dollars for three minutes!"

Loren nods. "You've got a point," he says. He reaches inside the Cadillac, takes the keys out of the ignition, and stuffs them into his pocket. "Follow me," he says. Inside the house, Loren hands the man the telephone and says, "Call your wife to come pick you up. Your car will be ready in a week."

David Weisz, a friend of mine with a reputation for artful negotiation and an office on Fifth Avenue, tells his children, "Always negotiate the price of products. Never negotiate the price of services. The services you get for half price are not the same services you get for full price."

Somewhere in Oklahoma is a knucklehead driving a Cadillac who would disagree with David Weisz. It is especially for knuckleheads like him that Mexican air traffic controllers offer two-peso weather reports. How about you? Would you prefer your car to be fixed in three minutes for fifty dollars or not fixed for five hundred? Do you want the two-peso weather report — or the fiiiiive-peso weather report? ❧

62

Is Failure the Key to Success?

HE PRESIDENT OF COCA-COLA said, "The moment you let avoiding failure become your motivator, you're down the path of inactivity. You can only stumble if you're moving. If you don't have a few failures, you're not taking enough chances. Nobody can be right all the time, and the big companies didn't become big by playing it safe."

During the formative years of Eastman Kodak, George Eastman criticized an associate in England for his overall timidity and lack of progress: "You, in England, are too cautious and afraid of making mistakes. We in the States make our mistakes and straighten them out before you even begin to make them."

Home-run slugger Babe Ruth was also the league leader in strikeouts during his career. Walt Disney was fired from an early job with an advertising agency because of a "singular lack of drawing ability," and Henry Ford went bankrupt before he built the Model T.

The secret, it seems, is to cheerfully embrace your failures and to count on your successes to outweigh them.

Take a chance. Risk failure. Change something that needs changing. ❧

63

Experiment!

HOMAS EDISON, inventor of the phonograph, light bulb, motion pictures, and many other things electric, once wrote an incredibly insightful memo to his salespeople. I've read the memo in Edison's own handwriting, and it convinces me of a genius that extended far beyond his understanding of electricity. Thomas Edison understood advertising, and Thomas Edison understood people.

Edison writes, "The art of selling goods is as difficult to acquire as any other art. The proper methods can be acquired only by a multiplicity of actual experiments, and the one who tries the greatest variety of experiments will become, finally, a master of the art."

The secret to becoming better at selling, it seems, is to experiment.

Contrary to what you might be thinking, an "experiment" is not an event. Experimentation is a perspective, a way of watching what happens and asking, "What have I learned?" then attempting to implement what you have learned, observing the result, and asking once more, "What have I learned?"

Throughout his long and productive life, Thomas Edison never quit experimenting. Never quit learning. Never quit becoming better. With this in mind, is it any wonder he discovered the wonderful things he found? ᑯᗷ

64

Hindsight Is 20/20

T HAS LONG BEEN MY HABIT to peruse old magazines and newspapers as I study advertising. Today I'll share a recent surprise discovery with you.

December 1931: The Great Depression was in full swing and a little magazine called the *Roycrofter* was being sold for twenty cents. In this particular issue, two very poignant thoughts came from staff writers trying to share an encouraging word during this time of financial hardship.

The first one wrote, "If you and I weren't smart enough in May 1929 to see the signs of the coming economic crash which was to occur in six short months, signs which were there in front of our eyes as plain as day, what makes us think we're smart enough to see today's signs of returning prosperity?"

I then turned to an article called "Five Minutes with Edison," written by a delightful fellow named Burton Bigelow, who said, "I have met Thomas Edison. My meeting lasted only a few minutes, but I have met Edison. My children shall hear of it, and my children's children. I shall probably tell the story over and over again, enlarging upon it each time, until I begin remembering things which never happened."

Bigelow makes a casual comment midway through the article, however, that not only startled me but immediately made me recall the earlier staff writer's comment about not being able to read "the signs which were there in front of our eyes as plain as day." Describing Edison's laboratory, he wrote, "Around the room were many young Japanese boys functioning as Edison's youthful laboratory assistants. Why mostly Orientals I never knew, but there they were."

There they were, indeed, Mr. Bigelow, and they're still here today. If you can hear me, Mr. Bigelow, those youthful laboratory assistants continued their studies long after old Tom Edison passed away, and it appears they will soon control the worldwide manufacture of electronic appliances. Each year there are fewer and fewer electronic items manufactured in the United States.

"The signs were there in front of our eyes as plain as day." What signs are in front of our eyes today? Success is often the result of noticing what others have overlooked. What might you be overlooking now? ❧

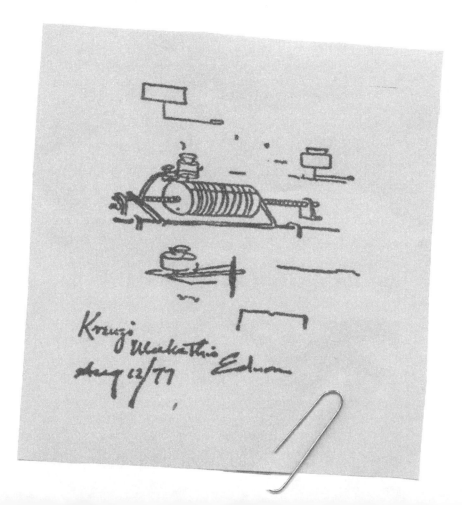

65

The Secret of Jack

THE DOCTOR SAID MY PHYSICAL SYMPTOMS were the result of a life-threatening level of stress. He said my body was convinced that I was engaged in mortal combat — a fight to the death. I was twenty-six.

Five months earlier, I had become general manager of a business that was much bigger than I was. At the office every morning by 7 AM and rarely home before the late evening news, I was working harder than I had ever worked in my life. Though the members of my staff were anxious to do their part, I was doing all the "important" things myself, and it seemed that far too many things were important. Does this story sound familiar to you?

Somewhere I had heard, "If you want a thing done right, you've got to do it yourself," and I had agreed. The result of this mindset was five months of crisis, pandemonium, chaos, and anarchy, ending in physical exhaustion and mental collapse. Now I was sitting on an examining table in a flimsy white robe that had a too-wide slit up the back.

Jack Kandel rescued me from that examining table when I hired him to be my boss. Jack taught me that a manager should never do anything himself. "It's not the manager's job," said Jack, "to actually do the work. It's the manager's job to see that all the work gets done, and that every employee gives the company the very best he or she has to give. It's the manager's job to make sure that everyone's needs are being met. A good manager is always available for a chat."

The he said something that stunned me: "The best managers are those who appear to be doing nothing. Nothing at all." It sounded crazy at the time, but today I'm convinced those were the words of a managerial genius.

Jack went on to say, "I've never once learned how to do an employee's job. I've always been afraid that if I knew how to do his job, I might be tempted to help him do it, or even to do it for him." When Jack noticed the puzzled look on my face, he summarized for me plainly: "When employees know that you are good at what they do, they tend to become increasingly helpless. When they know that you aren't able to do their jobs, they learn to do those jobs themselves, and you have a much happier company."

When there's a problem in your company, do you put on the Superman cape and come flying to the rescue? Or do you have enough confidence in your people to trust that they can do the right thing without you? Throughout his career, Jack Kandel was known as a jolly, happy man, and he never once failed to accomplish extraordinary things using very ordinary people.

I should know. I was one of them. ᑫᕼ

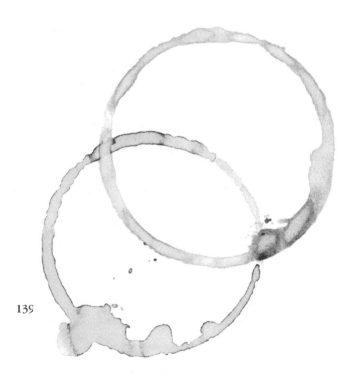

66
Pointing Chris Like a Gun

UST AS THE UPS OVERNIGHT PACKAGE hits the bottom of the post-office mailbox, Chris realizes what he has done. Most people would have simply shrugged and said, "UPS must have lost it." But Chris is not most people. Chris sits and waits for the nightly postal truck to come and collect the mail. When the driver begins spouting post-office regulations and tells Chris to go away, Chris politely says he will take it up with a postal supervisor.

Stopping at every blue box along the way, Chris follows the truck more than thirty-five miles to the Central Postal Facility, a huge compound surrounded by a tall, chain-link fence topped with barbed wire. When the guards open the gate to let the postal truck through, Chris nails his accelerator and shoots the gap. No time for explanations. Sliding to a stop in front of the main office, Chris runs inside only moments before the furious guards arrive on foot. There is quite a scene. Thirty minutes later, Chris hands my package to a man at United Parcel Service.

Jon tells me his flight number. I tell him Chris will meet him at the gate, not knowing that Chris will find a new sign in front of the metal detector: "Ticketed Passengers Only Beyond This Point." Not missing a step or pausing to think, Chris returns to his truck, where he stuffs his backpack full of things he finds behind the seat. He then digs through the airport trash until he finds an empty ticket folder, which he promptly tucks under his arm. With backpack and ticket folder in hand, Chris runs headlong across the parking lot, through the airport lobby, directly to the head of a long line. Shouting, "I'm sorry, everyone!" he tosses the backpack onto the conveyor belt and flashes the ticket jacket to the guard while diving through the metal detector. Never glancing back, Chris then runs down the concourse to the gate. As Jon steps off the plane, Chris is waiting. "So how was your flight?"

God help the person who stands between Chris and something I've asked him to do. If I send Chris to buy fruit and King Kong is guarding the bananas, call Hollywood. *King Kong Meets Chris* will be a box-office bonanza, but don't bet on the monkey to win. It is Chris who will come home with bananas.

Every business owner needs a Chris, but I'll warn you, there aren't nearly enough to go around. The secret of attracting a Chris and keeping it happy is knowing how to work with one. You see, a Chris will work with you, but never exactly for you, and a Chris cannot be badgered, bullied, frightened, bought, sold, bribed, or manipulated in any way. To attempt these things is to lose your Chris. And never tell a Chris *how* to do something. You should tell it only *what* you need done.

And when the thing is accomplished, don't ask a lot of questions. It would probably be better if you didn't know. ◪

Difficulties are things that show what men are.

— Epictetus

67

How Long Is Your Shadow?

T'S REALLY A DISADVANTAGE to have natural talent. The person with natural talent can make a job look so easy that people fail to appreciate it.

Another problem with being talented by nature is that you will find it nearly impossible to teach those who would learn from you. How can one teach what one knows instinctively and never had to learn?

The biggest problem with being naturally talented is that some idiot will decide to put you in charge. Sometimes the idiot is an employer who will ask you to run a department, but more often the idiot is you. "I'm so good at what I do, I think I'll go into business for myself."

I've seen this movie a hundred times. Let me tell you how it ends.

Your new business flourishes and thrives until it has grown to the length of your own shadow. The problem is that it doesn't stop there. Soon you have to work impossible hours just trying to keep up, but the business is now bigger than you are. Each week is filled with long hours, no days off, and phones ringing off the wall with customers calling to check on progress. You spend so much time trying to train the people you've hired that you finally decide it's easier simply to do it all yourself. But you can no longer do it all yourself, so you stare at the ceiling in the dark of night and ask, "Do I own a business, or does it own me?"

The polite knocking of opportunity has now become the relentless pounding of obligation. You were prepared to defeat a monster named Failure, but how can you overcome this beast called Success? As you look around in bewilderment, you realize

America is full of business people just like you, each of whom has built a company a little beyond the length of his shadow. The movie ends with a close-up of you staring into the camera, and the credits begin to roll as the light slowly fades into deep darkness around you.

Every time I watch this movie, I want to rewrite the ending. In my new finale, the owner doesn't give up on the people he's hired. He realizes the underlying problem is merely their lack of his natural talent, and he understands that someone else is better qualified to teach them. In the movie I would write, the business person invests in training for his people and develops procedures that allow extraordinary things to be accomplished by ordinary employees.

In my movie, the business becomes much, much bigger than the length of anyone's shadow.

How does your movie end? ∽

68

No Plan for Success

T WAS ALL A BIG MISTAKE. A shipment of pocket watches arrived at the train station addressed to a jeweler in Redwood Falls. The startled jeweler told the young railway agent that he never ordered the watches and refused to pay for them. The young railway agent, Richard Sears, decided to purchase the shipment of watches himself.

Evidently there was something magical about that shipment. Whoever accepted those watches was destined and fated to become rich. Either that, or a lowly railway agent named Richard Sears saw opportunity where others saw only problems.

The following year, Richard Sears moved to Chicago and ran an ad in the *Chicago Daily News*. "WANTED: Watchmaker with reference who can furnish tools. State age, experience, and salary required. ADDRESS T39, Daily News." An Indiana lad, Alvah Roebuck, answered the ad, never suspecting it to be the luckiest day of his life. Sears made him a partner, and Sears, Roebuck and Co. was born. Like the jeweler in Redwood Falls, however, Roebuck had little need for adventure and resigned from the company just a few years after responding to the classified ad.

Alvah Roebuck and the jeweler from Redwood Falls each had a plan for success, and the dreams of Richard Sears had no place in those plans. The jeweler was a jeweler. He didn't order any watches. Watches had no place in his plan. "Send the watches back." Roebuck was a watchmaker. His plan was to fix watches. Roebuck's plan had no place for a mail-order company, so he briskly stepped away. Richard Sears was a lowly railway agent who had no plan for watches, no plan for a direct-mail company, no plan for success at all. Richard Sears's only plan was to seek opportunities where others had found only problems. Sears would find a need, then fill it.

The cliff is high, but the view is beautiful. Will you walk near the edge with Richard Sears, or will you settle for a postcard from the tourist shop? If you choose to get in line for the postcard, buy a couple extra and send them to Alvah Roebuck and the jeweler in Redwood Falls. Write, "Having a great time, wish you were here," and sign it, "Richard Sears." &

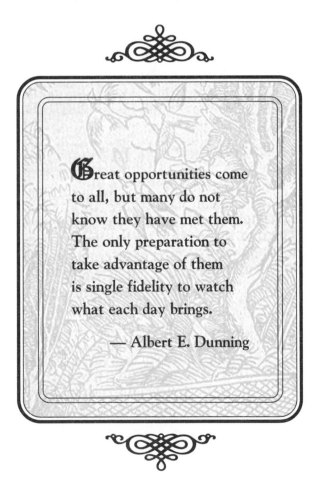

Great opportunities come
to all, but many do not
know they have met them.
The only preparation to
take advantage of them
is single fidelity to watch
what each day brings.

— Albert E. Dunning

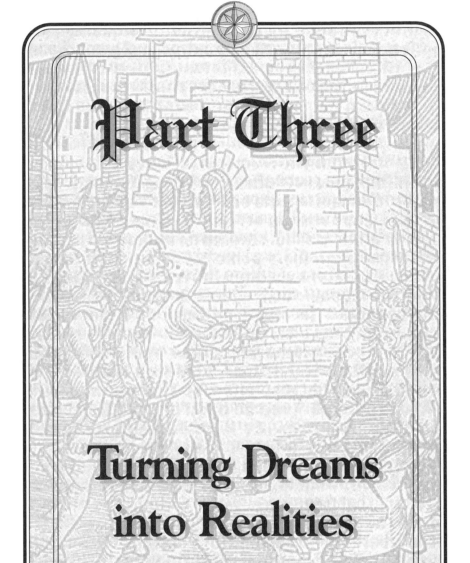

Part Three

Turning Dreams into Realities

69

Congratulations, You Won the Lottery!

INCOLN, NEBRASKA. Valencia Mueller stops at Wagner's Food Pride and buys a single lottery ticket. She wins. "I had trouble catching my breath," she says. "This only happens in dreams or in the movies, not in real life."

I think she overreacted.

Even if Valencia Mueller had won the ultimate payoff against odds of 54,979,155 to 1, it would have been no big deal, because Valencia had already won a much bigger lottery against much greater odds. Valencia Mueller had been born.

I asked Ryan J. Sokol of the statistics department at Texas A&M University to calculate the odds of a specific individual being born. Ryan estimated the total number of fertile men and women in the world, calculated the number of different genetic possibilities a man might contribute, adjusted for the number of hours of female fertility each month, then factored in a long list of other considerations. The bottom line of Ryan's lengthy report to me said, "The chance that you, meaning exactly you, would ever be born are 1 in 1.3 times ten to the twenty-ninth power."

In other words, 130,000,000,000,000,000,000,000,000,000 to 1. You and I, my friend, are two incredibly, amazingly, unbelievably lucky people. We both won the genetic lottery!

Compared with the odds against being born, the odds are very good that you will be elected president of the United States. Those odds are only 115,191,743 to 1.

You have already won a lottery more amazing than human-kind could ever devise. You have already been awarded a prize far richer than anything the world has to give.

You are alive. You are here. Make the most of it. ♈

The finger of God
never leaves identical fingerprints.

— Stanislaus Lec

70
Run with the BIG Dogs?

THE POWER OF ATOMIC ENERGY fades to insignificance when you've seen what I've seen. Nuclear vision is a power more awesome than nuclear fission.

Nuclear vision is a force that allows ordinary people to accomplish the impossible. A leader who radiates nuclear vision makes the people around him radioactive.

John F. Kennedy showed us nuclear vision when he said, "I'm going to put a man on the moon. Do you want to help?" The Rev. Martin Luther King Jr. shared his nuclear vision from the steps of the Lincoln Memorial, where he shouted, "I have a dream!" and the nation became radioactive with that dream. The men who sailed with Columbus were willing to risk falling off the edge of the world because of Columbus's nuclear vision of a round earth. Kennedy, King, and Columbus were all leaders with vision.

When undertaking any endeavor, vision is the ability to see the end from the beginning, and leadership is the ability to communicate that vision to the people around you, to accurately describe what you sincerely believe will happen. Visionary leadership is not a matter of genius — it's a matter of courage. Being a visionary leader requires that you risk the ridicule of others. You risk becoming a laughingstock. You risk being ignored.

If a visionary leader such as Kennedy or King or Columbus knew what you know and had your job, what do you think he would do?

Do it. Share with the people around you the secret dream you carry. Risk the ridicule of those who say it can't be done. Risk being wrong. The people who get radioactive will sail with you to the edge of the world.

Christopher Columbus asked men to sail west to find the East with him. JFK asked men to fly where there was no air. Following in the footsteps of his namesake, Martin Luther King Jr. challenged the status quo by denouncing practices that were unacceptable. Bicycle mechanic Wilbur Wright, retail merchant Richard Sears, abolitionist author Harriet Beecher Stowe, car builder Henry Ford, and women's suffragist Susan B. Anthony each dreamed of doing the impossible, and with nuclear vision they accomplished it.

Will you run with these big dogs, or will you stay on the porch? The choice is yours. The world has only players and spectators. Which are you?

All men dream, but not equally. They who dream by night in the dark recesses of their minds wake in the day to find that it is vanity. But the dreamers of the day are dangerous people, for they act out their dreams with open eyes to make them possible.

— T. E. Lawrence

71

Ted and the Redhead of 1886

 EW YORK CITY, 1886: As dock workers unload crates containing the Statue of Liberty, a young railway agent named Richard Sears is launching the company that will bring catalog shopping to America. In Atlanta, John Pemberton is mixing his first batch of Coca-Cola, and across the water, Gottlieb Daimler is tightening the last bolt on the world's first automobile.

Cars, catalogs, Coca-Cola, and the Statue of Liberty simultaneously come into existence in 1886. But what is the year's big news? According to *Manufacturer and Builder*, the leading monthly journal of innovation and change, the big news in New York isn't the Statue of Liberty but the scandal over the proliferation of overhead electric lines. Among the most important discoveries chronicled in the journal this year is a new way to color bricks red. The leaders of American industry are blind to the changes happening all around them. But not so the people.

America in 1886 is like a girl in adolescence, old enough to see glimpses of the woman she will become and anxious to complete the transformation. Her parents, the wealthy aristocrats who rule her thirty-eight states, are completely unprepared for the strong will of this redheaded teenage daughter.

The girl called America can't understand why the poor seem to have no rights. She is troubled by the fact that women have no vote, and she believes blacks deserve the same respect as whites. America in 1886 is a whirlwind redhead in need of a boyfriend who can keep up with her.

She finds him in Teddy Roosevelt. America falls in love with Teddy the moment she hears him say, "When they call the roll in the Senate, the senators do not know whether to answer 'present' or 'not guilty.' "

Teddy is a renegade Republican. His is the party of the rich, but Teddy is a man of the people. Teddy says to them, "The government is us; we are the government, you and I." When the Republicans become fearful of Teddy's wild ideas and his popularity among the commoners, they decide to bury him in the ultimate political grave: they make him the vice-presidential running mate to Stick-in-the-Mud McKinley. Shortly after the pair are elected, McKinley is assassinated. Teddy the Rough Rider is now president of the United States, and America loves it.

Immediately upon taking office, Teddy invites Booker T. Washington to dinner in the White House, and white rage is ignited across the South. Teddy says, "If I have erred, I err in company with Abraham Lincoln." With a smile that makes you feel he must have the teeth of a walrus, Teddy continues, "I am only an average man but, by George, I work harder at it than the average man."

When America was born in 1776, only rich, white males were allowed any hope. Then a mischievous cowboy swept America off her feet, and the land between Mexico and Canada has never been the same. ❧

Democracy is based upon the conviction that there are extraordinary possibilities in ordinary people.

— Harry Emerson Fosdick

72
Willie and His Bank Balance

T HAS LEFT ME WITH NOTHING TO HOPE FOR, **with** nothing definite to seek or strive for. Inherited wealth is a real handicap to happiness." So states William K. Vanderbilt, grandson of Cornelius "Commodore" Vanderbilt. Apparently Willie believes that the only way a person can measure success is by the size of his bank balance.

What a shame! Here's a man with the resources to attempt anything his imagination can conceive, and he has no dreams, aspirations, or goals that are bigger than him and his little bank account.

Willie's moanings underscore the importance of a question Pennie and I ask all our friends: "How will you measure success?"

Does anything loom bigger on the horizon of your mind than money? If your answer is no, I fear you will have a sad life. Yet if you have a dream whose accomplishment means more to you than cash, chances are you will enjoy the pursuit of that dream immensely, regardless of whether you ever achieve it.

If you aren't happy with the money you have now, what makes you think you'll be happier with more? If you believe **money is** a way of keeping score, you have condemned yourself to run forever, gasping for breath, in a race without a finish line. The race for more is a race in which there is never a winner.

Patrick Henry dreams of a free American nation. Orville and Wilbur Wright dream of flying like birds in the sky. Susan B. Anthony dreams of women voting like men. John F. Kennedy dreams of walking on the moon.

What dream fills the landscape of your imagination? If you cannot answer immediately, don't despair. Dreams quickly take root when their seeds are planted by one who has taken the time to care.

Look around you and care about the things you see. Your dream will sprout soon enough. There are many things bigger than money, Willie. Open your eyes and look around. ✑

Every affluent father wishes he knew how to give his sons the hardships that made him rich.

— Robert Frost

73

Not All the Rich Are Whiners, Willie

ILLIAM K. VANDERBILT SR. was a forgettable man, best remembered for whining that "inherited wealth is a real handicap to happiness."

Piffle, Willie. You simply have no imagination. Your own son proves it.

Willie Vanderbilt II is a young man fascinated with automobiles. He's often seen covered in grease with an entire engine spread out around him. In 1904, young Willie outruns Henry Ford to set a new world speed record, ninety-two miles per hour. Later in the year, Willie II holds the first Vanderbilt Cup Auto Race and single-handedly changes the course of American automaking.

Before the Vanderbilt Cup, American cars are merely motorized buggies moving not much faster than a horse can trot. By offering a first prize of nearly one million dollars (by today's standards), Willie II inspires more than three thousand entrepreneurs to leap to the task of manufacturing stronger, better, faster cars. The race is discontinued after its seventh year, because the crowds of more than 400,000 spectators can no longer be safely controlled.

Immediately following his final Vanderbilt Cup Auto Race, Willie II begins building himself a home. The house is only a cottage at first, obviously designed for solitude rather than glittering parties. Eagle's Nest is noted primarily for its excellent wharf and boathouse. Willie II's heart, mind, and energy have now turned to sea journeys and to marine life in all its strange and wonderful forms. Each day is to be a new adventure in the waters of the deep. Before his death in 1942, Willie II discovers sixty-eight species of ocean life previously unknown to science.

In his will, he shows generosity and optimism: "It is my desire and purpose that . . . Eagle's Nest become a public park and museum and as such be devoted in perpetuity to the use, education, and enjoyment of the public."

I am convinced that Willie II would have been happy regardless of his financial circumstances. I am equally convinced that his forgettable father would have been a whiner had he been born destitute, middle class, modestly wealthy, or Martian.

What about you? Will you follow the example of Willie the Forgettable and blame your unhappiness on your circumstances? Or will you wake up each morning like Willie the Adventurer and shout, "Oh, good morning! What a beautiful day!" ❧

No great man ever complains
of want of opportunity.

— Ralph Waldo Emerson

74

But What about Grandpa Cornelius?

ILLIE II'S GREAT-GRANDFATHER, Cornelius Vanderbilt, was in the first grade the year George Washington died. Five years later, Cornelius quit school at age eleven and set out to make his mark on the world.

When he was sixteen, Cornelius Vanderbilt borrowed his mother's life savings to buy a little sailboat to haul passengers and freight between Staten Island and New York City. Hungry, focused, and efficient, Vanderbilt quickly dominated the business and broke his competitors. His little boating enterprise became known as the Staten Island Ferry. By the time he was forty, his ships were hauling passengers and freight to ports all along the Atlantic coast, earning him the nickname "Commodore."

Since passengers and freight were the Commodore's business, it was only natural that he would buy up struggling railroads and turn them around. The difference between Vanderbilt and his predecessors was that his trains ran on schedule and the service was excellent. His New York Central Railroad quickly grew to become the nation's largest enterprise. During the Panic of 1873, Vanderbilt gave jobs to thousands by ordering the construction of Grand Central Station in New York City.

Cornelius Vanderbilt offered better service and lower prices than his competitors, but these are not the things that made him wealthy. The characteristics that made him one of the richest men in the world were best described by a friend:

> The largest employer of labor in the United States, he despised all routine office work; kept his figures in a vest-pocket book; ate sparingly; never speculated in stocks; never refused to see

a caller; rose early; read *Pilgrim's Progress* every year; and, for diversion, played whist and drove his trotters whenever he could.

Cornelius Vanderbilt did not offer better service and lower prices so that he might become rich. He became rich because he loved hauling passengers and freight, and because he did it very, very well.

Why do you do what you do? Is it for the money alone, or is it because you love to do it well? Wealth is not a destination, not a sparkling city on a hill. Wealth is simply a by-product of passion. You will become truly rich only when you learn to love what it is you do.

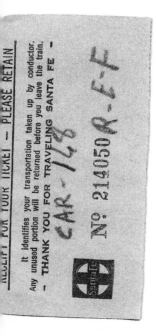

Success is a journey,
not a destination.

— Ben Sweetland

75

Sue's Little Boy

SUE DROPPED OUT OF SCHOOL when she learned she was pregnant. She had just turned sixteen. No education, no skills, no money, few friends. Sue had a little boy.

Sue never taught her little boy about the importance of education. She never warned him about falling in love too soon. Sue told her little boy only that the world was looking for people on whom it could depend, and that he should be one of those people. And every day, as he stepped out the door to begin his long walk to school, Sue would say, "You're an extremely smart little boy and things come easily to you. You can be anything you want to be. Opportunity is all around you." Then she would go off to the huge place where she worked putting files in alphabetical order.

The little boy's grades were only average, but because his family was poor, the government offered to pay his way through college. He went for a while but didn't find it interesting, so he came home and asked his girlfriend to marry him, still believing that he was a smart little boy and that opportunity was all around him.

All this was many years ago.

The people she worked for quickly learned that they could depend on Sue and suspected that she might be capable of more than putting files in alphabetical order. They liked the fact that Sue could see solutions where others saw only problems. She was promoted from level to level.

One day, when the company had a department in turmoil, Sue was given the job of restructuring, reorganizing, and remotivating its people. Soon Sue's department was the smoothest running in the entire organization. Then another department was in trouble, and Sue was again called to the rescue. Over the years, she was given each of the company's departments at least once.

Sue retired a rich woman at the age of fifty-four and announced that she would begin a new career in fashion modeling. Sue's friends laughed till their sides hurt, because Sue looked very much like the average fifty-four-year-old woman. "That's my point, exactly," said Sue. "Fifty-four-year-old women don't want to see how clothes will look on twenty-year-old supermodels. They want to see how clothes will look on a woman who is shaped like they are."

Several modeling agencies laughed her out the door, but Sue still believed that opportunity was all around her. Today she travels America and Europe as a television spokesmodel, a runway model, and a catalog fashion model, and her little boy makes more money than the president of the United States, because his mother taught him to see opportunity everywhere, and because people learned they could depend on him.

Sad stories don't have to have sad endings — and by the way, this story is true.

Haven't you heard? This is America. ❧

$$O$$pportunity is as scarce as oxygen;
men fairly breathe it and do not know it.

— Doc Sane

76

The Song of the Weasel

AVE YOU EVER LOOKED CLOSELY at a weasel? The weasel is an obvious first cousin to the rat, and in today's business climate, it is becoming very important that you know how to deal with him.

Weasels are quick to ask for help but slow to give it; a weasel can wiggle out of anything. "I don't remember saying that." "Sorry, I've got other plans." "I'd love to help but I've got a bad back." "I left my wallet at home."

Weasels cannot be trusted, but don't bother trying to escape them. Weasels are everywhere, incessantly singing their sad little song: "If Only." "If only I had a better education." "If only my boss liked me better." "If only I had married someone else." "If only I had invested in Chrysler when it was fifty cents a share."

Weasels specialize in whining, but they are equally good at blame shifting. According to the weasel, no mistake has ever been his fault. "I thought Bob was taking care of that." "You should have told me sooner." "Why didn't someone remind me?" "You should never have asked me in the first place — it's not my job."

Have you seen the TV commercial for Mennen Skin Bracer? Looking into the mirror, a man slaps himself hard with one hand, then with the other. Remember what he says? "Thanks, I needed that."

Well, the truth of the matter is, there's a little weasel in all of us, and that weasel needs to be slapped. When your ears hear your lips start to sing the song of the weasel, you must learn to immediately slap the weasel within.

Everyone admires the hardy individual who can look into the mirror of his soul and give the weasel within the cold, hard slap known as "remembrance of obligation." If the first slap doesn't subdue the weasel, a second slap, "loyalty," will get him every time.

Slappers believe in helping others; weasels help only themselves. Slappers are good at getting things done; weasels, at making excuses. Slappers are dependable, but so are weasels — they'll let you down every time. Everybody loves a weasel slapper, but nobody likes a weasel.

Which one is winning the battle in your mirror? &

He who overcomes others is strong, but he who overcomes himself is mightier.

— John Henry Patterson

77

Strangers on the Beach

T IS A COLD THURSDAY MORNING in December, and I've had three days of poor fishing. Water is freezing in hoofprints on the road. I am looking toward the sea, unsure whether I will fish, when I see that the strange brothers are still camped out on the beach. I guess crazy people don't feel cold like the rest of us.

As I walk toward the camp, I am intercepted by little Johnny Ward, who falls into step beside me. We greet the brothers and are offered coffee, which we gladly accept. Johnny Ward, spying a box filled with eggs, asks one of the men where they got so many. "Didn't you notice the small hen running about?" says the man to Johnny. "That hen lays eight to ten eggs a day!" I know the man is joking, but Johnny runs off to find the miraculous hen.

The brothers are building a machine that will, they say, fly like a bird and carry them into the sky. I warm my hands around my coffee cup and quickly change the subject. "Woolworth says he's going to build the tallest building in the world. What do you think about that?" The quiet brother says, over his shoulder, "I think that's a lot of nickels and dimes."

He turns and shows me a box on three legs and asks if I can make a photograph. I tell him I've never done it, but that I'm willing to try. He sets up the three-legged box and points it toward the beach. "Just squeeze this bulb when I pass in front of you."

The brothers' strange kite, all cloth and wires, has a motor that sounds like hail on a barn roof. I watch as it lumbers down the beach gaining speed. In a moment, it is in front of me.

I come to my senses sitting on the ground with a crowd gathered about me shouting, "Did you get it? Did you get it?"

I'm not sure what they mean. My brain has been foggy for several minutes, but I think I just saw a man fly into the sky. I'm not sure it really happened, and I'm afraid to ask. One of the men says, "The shutter is dropped. Let's see what he got."

The picture I've made will become the most famous photograph in the world. I have recorded the first moment of the first powered flight of a heavier-than-air flying machine. Orville and Wilbur tell me the name of John T. Daniels will forever be etched in history. I'm glad I didn't go fishing.

As the brothers help me to my feet, little Johnny Ward arrives to proclaim, "But it's only a common-looking chicken!" I am told that Johnny Ward will someday look into a magic window and watch a man stride the surface of the moon. I am told that all houses will have such windows in the future. ꙮ

Photo by John T. Daniels

78

Thumbing Through the Diary of a Genius

"OUR FIRST INTEREST BEGAN when we were children. Father brought home to us a small toy actuated by a rubber string which would lift itself into the air. We built a number of copies of this toy, which flew successfully." — Orville Wright

JUNE 1, 1900, FROM DAYTON, OHIO: "For the present, I have but little time for my aeronautical investigations, in fact I try to keep my mind off the subject during the bicycle season as I find that business is neglected otherwise." — Wilbur

SEPTEMBER 23, 1900, FROM KITTY HAWK: "I have not taken up the problem with the expectation of financial profit. Neither do I have any strong expectation of achieving the solution at the present time or possibly any time. My trip would be no great disappointment if I accomplish practically nothing." — Wilbur

FRIDAY, SEPTEMBER 26, 1902, FROM KITTY HAWK: "I put in part of the day constructing a death trap for a poor mouse that has been annoying us by prowling about our kitchen shelves at nights. We are now anxiously awaiting the arrival of the 'victim.'" — Orville

SATURDAY, SEPTEMBER 27, 1902, FROM KITTY HAWK: "At 11 o'clock last night I was awakened by the mouse crawling over my face. Will had advised me that I had better get something to cover my head, or I would have it 'chawed' off like Guillaume Mona had by the bear. I found on getting up that the little fellow had only come to tell me to put another piece of corn bread in the trap. He had disposed of the first piece. I have sworn 'vengeance' on the little fellow for this impudence and insult." — Orville

OCTOBER 18, 1903, FROM KITTY HAWK: "The wopper flying machine is coming on all right and will probably be done about November 1." — Wilbur

NOVEMBER 20, 1903, FROM KITTY HAWK: "While in the bicycle business we had become well acquainted with the use of hard tire cement for fastening tires on the rims. We had once used it successfully for repairing a stop watch after several watch smiths had told us it could not be repaired. If tire cement was good for fastening the hands on a stop watch, why should it not be good for fastening the sprockets on the propeller shaft of a flying machine?" — Orville

IN A WESTERN UNION TELEGRAPH to their father, December 17, 1903: "SUCCESS FOUR FLIGHTS THURSDAY MORNING ALL AGAINST TWENTY ONE MILE WIND STARTED FROM LEVEL WITH ENGINE POWER ALONE AVERAGE SPEED THROUGH AIR THIRTY ONE MILES LONGEST 57 SECONDS INFORM PRESS. HOME CHRISTMAS. ORVILLE"

> When Columbus discovered America he did not know what the outcome would be, and no one at that time knew; and I doubt if the wildest enthusiast caught a glimpse of what really did come from his discovery. In a like manner these two brothers have probably not even a faint glimpse of what their discovery is going to bring to the children of men.
>
> — Amos I. Root, January 1, 1905

Geniuses are just regular people, doing what they love. Do you love what you do? ॐ

79
Listening to Ted

ED WAS A CRUSTY OLD WAR VETERAN and a maestro of profanity. Born into a family long on children and short on money, Ted grew into a salty, mean, wily survivor. When I was fifteen, Ted hired me to do all the jobs in his steel shop that no self-respecting steelworker would touch. I was known as "Schoolboy." "Schoolboy! Scrub the #@^/* bathroom!" "Schoolboy! Mow the @#^/* lawn!" "Load the @/*#^ scrap metal, Schoolboy, and sell it to the ^/*@# junkyard!"

My favorite job was to load a thousand gallons of water onto Ted's truck and then drain it down a hole in Ted's front yard whenever his well ran dry. Looking back, I see the day Ted taught me to haul water as pivotal in my life.

We began by driving north forever, beyond the little farms at the edge of town, out past the industrial wasteland, to the dusty middle of Nowhere. The only business in sight was a little gas station with a rough, gravel parking lot, the last shred of a community long dead.

Ted parked under a tree at the edge of the gravel, and we got out of the truck together. "C'mere, Schoolboy! I'm going to teach you how to haul @^/*# water." Walking behind a pile of junk at the edge of the gravel, Ted emerged with a gigantic canvas hose, which he strapped to the opening of our homemade water tank. He then turned a hidden valve within the junk pile. I watched in amazement as gloriously bright, clean water began gushing into our tank.

During the silent ride home, Ted swerved into the left lane as though passing an invisible car. Being only a "schoolboy," I knew it wasn't proper for me to question Ted's driving, but curiosity got the best of me. "Look behind us," Ted answered. While I looked out the back window of the truck, Ted said, "You see that big elm with the branch that hangs over the road? Well, that branch is dead, and someday it's gonna fall." As I turned back around to stare quietly at the road ahead of us, Ted added, "And I don't want to be under it when it does."

Seeing that Ted was completely serious, I answered him as solemnly as I knew how. "Thanks for pointing that out, Ted, I'll try to remember it." Ted turned and looked at me as though he had only just noticed I was there. "Schoolboy, every living person has something he can teach you. Always find out what it is and let him teach it to you. Folks are happy to teach you valuable things if you'll only let 'em."

After a long silence, Ted spoke again. "Schoolboy, if you can find even one true friend in your life, you'll have done better than most . . . but you'll never find a true friend unless you're willing to be one." After another long pause, Ted continued: "Schoolboy, a true friend is someone who doesn't back away from you, even when it costs him."

We rode the remaining miles in silence, but I understood. Ted had shared his secret fear of the elm with me, and I had listened and not laughed, and a valve had opened. The day Ted taught me to haul water, I learned that beneath even the shabbiest gravel parking lot, one can find a wealth of hidden treasure. ❧

80

The Power of Encouragement

HEN I WAS NINETEEN, I spent every Saturday from 1 AM to 10 AM in the control room of a low-power, Christian radio station on the AM dial in Oklahoma. Our Saturday program line-up was mostly local guys with a message in their heart and thirty dollars in their pocket. Dick Bailey was one of those guys.

Nine hours came to about twenty dollars a week after taxes, but Pennie and I needed the money, so every Friday I would hurry home after eleven hours in a welding shop, sleep about five hours, then drive forty minutes to the radio station, where I would change tapes for the next nine hours. Lunchtime saw me staggering home to fall into bed. All this for twenty dollars a week — but I got to meet Dick Bailey.

Old enough to be my granddad, Dick Bailey came to the studio each Saturday morning about 5:30 to do his radio show, "Live from the Top of Inspiration Mountain." He would always close the show by announcing where he was going to have breakfast, and he'd invite anyone listening to join him.

When you change tapes once a week in the middle of the night on the number twenty-one station in a city of twenty-one stations, you are definitely the lowest form of life in broadcasting. Delivery men, the janitorial staff, and especially the part-timers at the FM station across the hall took great pleasure in ridiculing me. My incredibly low status was probably the reason Dick Bailey never failed to bring me a little gift each Saturday morning.

Dick worked as a salesman for Brown and Bigelow, an advertising specialties company. The first of Dick's many gifts to me was to say, "Roy, you're doing a fine job," as he pressed into my hand a little screwdriver, which I carry on my key chain to this very day. The next week it was "Roy, you're a hard worker, and I'm convinced you're going to be a great man someday." Then he handed me two Norman Rockwell prints, which Pennie still proudly displays in our dining room. One week, Dick told me a big company had placed a large order for ink pens, which had qualified them to receive a fifty-dollar, embossed-leather thesaurus. He said they didn't care about the thesaurus, so he was having it sent to me.

Dick Bailey believed in me long before *I* believed in me. His affirmations each week helped me bounce out of bed with a sense of mission and purpose. There might have been only fourteen people listening to my station, but one of them was Dick Bailey, and Dick cared whether I did a good job.

One Friday evening, Pennie and I opened our mail to find the most elegant leather thesaurus we had ever seen. Twelve hours later, as the morning clock approached 5:30, I walked from the control room to the parking lot to see if I could spot Dick getting out of his car. Finally, I walked back to the control room and turned the page of the program log to find a little note from the station manager: "Dick Bailey died in his sleep yesterday. Please play one of his prerecorded standby programs."

Each morning, as I unlock my office doors, a little screwdriver on my key chain quietly whispers, "Encourage the people around you today, for you never know who they might become, or what tomorrow may bring." ❧

81
Leaving Something on the Table

YRIL AND JOHN ARE NEGOTIATING. Cyril presses for one point too many and causes the mercury to reach the boiling point on John's annoyance thermometer. Noticing the change in mood, Cyril smiles and excuses himself by saying, "I just wanted to be sure I wasn't leaving anything on the table. You can't blame me for trying."

"Yes, Cyril, I can blame you for trying. I blame you because I was hoping we could both win, but now I see that I can never turn my back on you. I can never rest when you are near. You have revealed yourself to be the adversary you are. Thank you. I hope never to deal with you again as long as the earth revolves." Though these words are not spoken aloud, you can be sure they are carved in granite behind John's answering nod and smile.

Who, then, is the loser in this negotiation?

I believe there are times to leave something on the table. When you hope to do business with someone again, leave a little on the table. When you want a person to speak well of you, leave a little on the table. When you want superior service, leave a little more on the table. When you want to make someone your ally and your friend, be sure every deal is good for him, too, and change the deal when it's not.

If your own reputation and future business dealings are of no concern to you, the only thing you must do to prove yourself a hard-nosed businessman is squeeze the last drop out of every negotiation. It's easy to do! Just demand the very most for the very least in return. Grab and squeeze.

Becoming the person to whom others enjoy giving a bargain is more difficult. First, you must learn what the other person wants most out of the deal. Often there's an element of the transaction that's very important to him but about which you care very little. Once you've uncovered this "Achilles heel," do NOT dangle it like a carrot. Don't make him bargain for it at all. Make the concession immediately and with no strings attached, then with a smile ask plainly for the thing that's most important to you. Typically, a mutually beneficial relationship will result, and you'll also have gained a friend who will be there for you the next time you need him.

Will you maintain an adversarial posture and fight the whole world alone, or will you win an army of friends? No one stands long on the battlefield who has not built an army of friends.

To make an enemy your friend is easy. Simply do what a friend would do. ✄

I will destroy my enemies
by converting them to friends.

— Maimonides

82

Celebrate the Ordinary

 VERYONE HAS HEARD OF MURPHY'S LAW — "Whatever can go wrong, will go wrong." Who was this guy Murphy, anyway, and why do we quote him? Any fool can see that a great deal more unexpected good happens each day than unexpected bad. Bad news is reported by the media only because it is so rare. Good news is so abundant that it's rarely considered news at all.

Over the years, Murphy's whining has been published on enough calendars and printed on enough wall plaques that many Americans have adopted his twisted perspective as the foundation for their own world view. Sitting in warm homes, driving beautiful cars, and eating delicious meals, these misguided friends still believe, deep in their hearts, that "whatever can go wrong, will go wrong."

If we look for the bad in every situation, is there any doubt we will find it?

Our lives are like an unplanned picnic. We awaken to find ourselves surrounded by beautiful scenery, good friends, and excellent food. Shall you and I fill this bright day with challenging games and warm conversation, or would you prefer to complain about the ants and fret about the mosquitoes?

Take a moment to consider the abundance of good things in your life. Does anyone love you? Celebrate it. Is there anything you do well? Take pleasure in it. Is your health good enough to survive the day? Revel in it. If you want every day to be a happy day, you must learn to celebrate the ordinary.

As a little boy in an Oklahoma Sunday school, I remember being taught to sing a song with a powerful final verse:

> Count your blessings
> Name them one by one
> Count your many blessings
> See what God has done.

Murphy must never have had the chance to attend an Oklahoma Sunday school. What a pity. His life could have been so different.

There is no cure for birth or death
save to enjoy the interval.

— George Santayana

83
Murphy Finally Figures It Out

HE PLATITUDE KNOWN AS MURPHY'S LAW, "Whatever can go wrong, will go wrong," was actually Murphy's third law in a series of eleven such observations. To satisfy your curiosity, Murphy's first law is "Nothing is as easy as it looks," and his next nine make increasingly cynical statements about the nature of the universe and the futility of life, reaching a crescendo in Murphy's tenth law, "Mother Nature is a bitch."

I'm convinced the immortal Murphy intended to stop at an even ten laws, but a startling revelation occurred to him in later years, leading him to formulate his insightful eleventh law. Here he seems to have found an entirely new perspective. Number eleven causes me to believe Murphy finally figured it out.

The real problem with society is people. (No, this is not Murphy's eleventh, it's simply my own observation.) It seems to me that everyone is frantically searching for someone who can supplement his shortcomings, and in the absence of such a savior, we rage in fury at the cosmos.

I am convinced this is why opposites attract. All of us have areas in which we are weak, and we're instinctively attracted to any person whose strengths are in those areas. Conversely, we have no patience with any person who's weak in an area where we are strong. A person who is always punctual has no respect for those who are habitually late. A thrifty person considers a liberal man foolish, and the liberal man calls the thrifty person "stingy." Yet the world needs them both.

Have you ever walked into an establishment and read the sign, "A lack of preparation on your part does not constitute an emergency on my part"? This is just another indication of how the world is looking for someone who will come to the rescue and of how few of us want to be that person.

Rescuing people from the results of their own foolishness is really what customer service is all about. Customers rarely obey the rules. They expect you to rescue them whenever they do something stupid. Will you be a "rescuer," known far and wide for customer service, or will you steadfastly insist that your customers follow proper procedures?

Not only does every cloud have a silver lining, but it has a beautiful sky above it and a warm earth beneath. The world God gave us is flawless. It's you and I who need some work.

Oh, yes, Murphy's eleventh law? "It is impossible to make anything foolproof, because fools are so ingenious."

Do a new thing today. Rescue a fool who doesn't deserve it. Tomorrow you may need him to rescue you from a shortcoming of your own. ❧

Be thankful not only that you are an individual but also that others are different. The world needs all kinds, but it also needs to respect and use that individuality.

— Donald A. Laird

84

When in Pain

Y DOG, STUBBY, WAS HIT BY A CAR when I was five years old. The image of my father stepping through the door with Stubby in his arms will forever be etched in my mind. I went into shock. Stubby was my best friend.

Stubby wasn't dead, but his leg was badly broken and there was quite a bit of blood. As I stretched out my hand to stroke Stubby's head, my father took a step backward. "Wait," said Dad. "When a creature is in pain, he'll often bite whoever is near."

This week I received a long, vicious letter from a complete and total stranger. He claimed to be an expert in psychoanalysis and spent several paragraphs twisting his psychological knife into my guts. The malice of his letter was truly astonishing, as I had done nothing to deserve it.

Rage sharpened my wit to a razor's edge and focused my mind to write the supremely caustic response. I lifted my pen as though it were an ice pick I would drive into his heart. Then I recalled the words of my father.

I began my note by apologizing for what I had unwittingly done, then added, "I fear, however, that you have overanalyzed. None of the motivations of which you accuse me ever once crossed my mind." I assured the man that whatever annoyance I had caused was completely unintentional and closed by asking him to forgive me.

Respect for his privacy prohibits me from revealing the details of his reply, but I will share the two pivotal sentences: "Actually, my psychology background is a personal issue, as my son is an autistic seven-year-old. I have kept up my studies of brain function primarily for his well-being."

Stubby hobbled around the yard for a few weeks with an awkward cast around his leg. Afterwards, Stubby was fine.

I think, perhaps, there are other wounds less easily mended. 🙷

85

Paul's Adopted Son

AUL COMPTON HAD A WIFE AND FOUR DAUGHTERS, and in later years, a fourteen-year-old son added himself to the dinner table. That son was me. My own mother was a great cook and she loved me like crazy, but Mom had to work full time and she had a lot to do in the evenings, so I fell into the habit of showing up at Paul's house every night around suppertime.

Paul Compton is the kindest and best man I've ever known. Paul understands the difference between "doing" and "being," so he never once asked, "What do you want to do when you grow up?" Paul felt he knew who I was going to be, and for Paul, that was enough.

Many nights after dinner, Paul's youngest daughter and I would get up from the table and leave on separate dates, but after our dates we would often seek one another's advice. Over the next four years, she had a long string of boyfriends and I had a long string of girlfriends, but when she wasn't on a date with a boyfriend and I wasn't on a date with a girlfriend, Paul's daughter and I were most likely together, usually about five nights a week.

It know it sounds insane, but Paul's daughter and I went at least a thousand places together without it ever crossing my mind to hold her hand as we were walking.

Somewhere near the end of our senior year, as she and I returned from buying a root beer across town, I turned off the ignition, looked at her, and said, "I recently realized that I enjoy being with you more than anyone else in the world, and that makes it difficult for us to be friends anymore, because it would be torture for me to keep seeing you every night if I thought there was ever a chance it would end." I had never once kissed Paul's daughter good night. Six months later we were married.

A whole generation of American kids grew up being asked, "What do you want to do when you grow up?" as though it would be the most important question we would ever face. It wasn't. We learned we could easily and painlessly change careers throughout the course of our lives. Not one of my childhood pals is currently involved in the career for which he studied. Now that I have boys of my own, I've elected not to quiz them about their choice of careers.

Should any person ever ask my sons what is important to their father, I'll wager that my boys will be able to recite it verbatim. "Boys, when you're ready to marry, don't marry a person who has high and lofty expectations of you. Don't marry the girl you've struggled to impress. Marry the girl you always thought of as a sister, the one who knows you as you really are. Marry the girl who has seen your every fault and weakness but likes to be with you just the same. Boys, when you're ready to get married, I hope you'll marry your best friend." ❧

The universe is full of magical things,
patiently waiting for our wits to grow sharper.

— Eden Philpotts

86

Thinking with Your Heart

YOU'VE HEARD THESE PHRASES: "a woman's intuition," "female intuition," "a mother's intuition."

"Exactly what," you ask, "is intuition?"

Essentially, intuition is the ability to think with your heart instead of your head. It's the ability to come to the right conclusion when you haven't been given enough information. In a nutshell, intuition is what makes humans smarter than machines.

It's also what makes women smarter than men. Notice that I said "smarter," not "more intelligent." Men will often focus the mind but ignore the heart. Women make this mistake far less often.

Intellect is linear, putting facts in columns and rows, while intuition is nonlinear, putting all the facts in a big bowl, then stirring them together like soup, watching to see what might "connect." The intuitive person can rarely convince the intellectual of anything, because intuition seldom comes with proof. Intuitive people aren't completely sure why they know what they know.

Intellect may not fail as often as intuition, but it doesn't win as often, either. Great leaders have intuition. Explorers have intuition. Inventors have intuition. It is intuition that tells them how to go where none has ever been.

Intellect is to be cherished. Please don't think I'm trying to diminish it. I'm merely urging you to give intuition the credit it deserves. I hope to give you the courage to follow your heart. Sometimes the thing that makes the least sense is exactly the right thing to do. ◆

later e
Noneth
nd subseque.
nder fire.
What is the
etween the French

**The human race
is governed
by its imagination.**

Napoleon Bonaparte

87

The Canyon of Wile E. Coyote

ILE E. COYOTE IS A MENSA GENIUS whose only thought is to catch the Roadrunner. With the unlimited resources of Acme Corporation at Wile E.'s disposal, one might easily consider the Roadrunner doomed. But it never seems to work out that way.

Wile E. Coyote is a victim of overplanning. It is this over-planning, not the Roadrunner, that lands Wile E. at the bottom of the canyon.

Overplanning assumes that a plan can be and should be prepared for every possible contingency. Unfortunately, life doesn't come in that small a package. It's easy to respond to actual circumstances, but impossible to respond to imaginary ones.

Overplanning comes naturally to any person with a highly developed intellect and a morbid fear of failure. Western society has placed such a premium on success that few of us can bear the thought of failure. Yet failure is the key to success.

The person most likely to succeed is the one who recognizes the temporary nature of failure and consequently has no fear of it — a person who knows that each failure brings him one step closer to success.

In life there is no rule that says, "Three strikes and you're out." We can stay in the batter's box until we grow weary of swinging or fall over dead. I say, "Swing till you hit."

Isn't it time to quit being scared? Relax and enjoy the game! (Beep! Beep!) ⌇

88

Milestones and Dreams

 HAVE ALWAYS HAD VERY LONG ARMS. Because of this, I spent the first thirty-two years of my life with the cuffs turned back on my sleeves. In my mind, this made me look rugged. In reality, my only alternative was to button my cuffs two inches above my wrists and look exactly like Jethro Bodean.

The day I bought a shirt that fit was one of the most momentous days of my life. I worked thirty-two years to reach the point where I could spend enough money to buy a shirt that fit without having to feel guilty. Shirts with long arms cost more than a shirt should cost. With a wife and two kids, I could never buy a long-arm shirt with money that might have been better spent on other things. Today I have nine times more shirts than pants, but Pennie understands.

As a kid, I was always impressed when a friend would open his kitchen cupboard to get a drinking glass and reveal two dozen matching glasses inside. If his family's bath towels were also a matched set, these people stood on the very pinnacle of Mt. Affluent. Matching towels and drinking glasses spoke of having more money than was needed.

When I was twenty, Pennie and I were conned into attending a multilevel marketing meeting. The multilevel evangelist was amazing. He made all in the room feel that wealth, power, and glory were right at their fingertips, if only they would open their eyes to see. He was a powerful speaker, but I felt betrayed by his phony offer — "I want you to come over so we can get to know each other better" — when all he really wanted was for us to sell soap for him. So we didn't join. But I did agree with one thing he said. When he asked, "Aren't you tired of reading restaurant menus from right to left?" I had to answer in the affirmative.

Someday I want to own an office building with a view that will take your breath away. Someday I want to write a book you can find in any bookstore. Someday I want to produce a movie. But if none of these things ever happens, I'll continue to live a contented man, because I'm the guy in the restaurant wearing a shirt that fits, recklessly ordering whatever I want. Back home, my drinking glasses are all alike and my bath towels are a matched set. From here on out, anything else is gravy.

Too much has been written about financial goal setting in business, and too little about how we can measure success in more meaningful ways. So let me ask *you:* What are your milestones and dreams?

You see things; and you say Why?
But I dream things that never were;
and I say Why not?

— George Bernard Shaw

89

Creativity Is an Inert Gas

OUR NERVES ARE ON EDGE; you jump at the slightest sound; you've been pushed beyond your comfort zone; too many people are expecting too much of you; the pendulum of your life swings wildly out of control; your soul cries out for peace.

Finally, the crisis passes. You luxuriate in an atmosphere of no demands. Life's once flailing pendulum returns to its graceful arc. Your life feels centered again.

This moment of emotional recovery is the best possible time to think about problems you have not been able to solve. Moments of great, creative insight always follow the times of greatest stress. It's a law of the universe.

Think of creativity as an inert gas, a substance unique. An inert gas cannot enter into compounds with other substances because, in each of its atoms, the outer ring of electrons is completely full. An inert gas is completely stable and cannot be changed.

Unless you jolt it with too much stimulation.

Pass a current through an inert gas and a single electron in the outer ring of each atom will be pushed into an orbit where it does not belong. But it cannot stay there. As the electron falls back into its proper place, the excess energy will be released as light.

This is a miracle witnessed nightly on ten million street corners in America. Without argon and mercury vapor street lights, America would be a very dark place, indeed. Without the radiant beauty of neon, we would be a much less colorful people.

Recovery from overstimulation is a magical moment. As each crisis dissipates and your emotional electrons return to their proper orbits, don't close your eyes to the light.

Use it for all it's worth. ❧

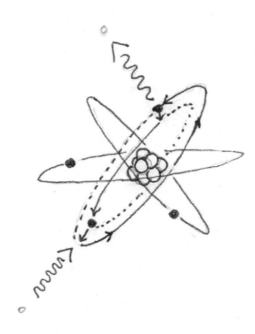

90

Fingerprints of God

HEERFUL CHARLIE ONCE TOLD ME, "There's no feeling like the one you get when you know you're in the right place at the right time, doing the right thing in the right way." My friend David Dalgliesh knows exactly what Charlie is saying, but David calls it "finding your sweet spot in life."

David and I have a mutual friend named Tom Pelton who has found his sweet spot in life. It was only 6 PM but already dark when Tom walked into my office one January and said, "I've decided to start a church for people who aren't religious." Had it been anyone but Tom, I would have said, "That's the dumbest thing I've ever heard in my life." But it was Tom, so I said, "Sounds like just the thing this town needs."

Tom then showed me a letter he planned to mail to each of the ten thousand homes in his zip code. The opening line of the letter said, "You believe in God. It's Christians you're not sure about, right?" I warned Tom the letter would probably offend a lot of ministers, but Tom said, "Roy, those people are already in church. This letter is for all the people who aren't."

Since Tom didn't want to pull people away from regular churches, he decided his services would be on Saturday nights. The next day he leased a metal building that sat way back off the road under some trees. The parking lot was exactly the kind of spot favored by drug dealers after dark.

When Tom woke up on Saturday, it occurred to him that his parking lot had no lights and that it would be pitch dark by the time services started. Knowing the building would appear ominous and forbidding without any exterior lights, Tom decided to try to rig up something before nightfall. He scurried around and borrowed lamps, ladders, and extension cords. When he pulled into his parking lot with this ridiculous assortment of gear, a big city utilities truck turned in behind him. The driver walked up to Tom's window and told Tom that long ago the city had scheduled this particular parking lot to get four street lights. He asked if Tom would "please try to stay out of the way, because we need to have these lights up and working before dark."

When Tom sees things fall into place with an ease that suggests his path has been prepared for him, he believes he is seeing the fingerprints of God, and there is nothing quite so encouraging as finding them.

Why don't you look for the fingerprints of God in your own life today? I promise you, they're all around you. ◈

91

If at First You Don't Succeed . . .

IT'S 1848. NINE IRISHMEN have been captured, tried, and convicted of treason against Her Majesty, the Queen. They are sentenced to death. The men's names are Charles Duffy, John Mitchell, Morris Lyene, Pat Donahue, Thomas McGee, Richard O'Gorman, Thomas Meagher, Michael Ireland, and Terrence McManus.

As the judge is about to pronounce their sentence, he asks if there is anything they would like to say. Meagher steps forward and speaks for the group. "My Lord, this is our first offense. If you will be easy with us this once, we promise, on our word as gentlemen, to try to do better next time. And next time — you can be certain we'll not be such fools as to get caught!"

The embarrassed and infuriated judge sentences them to be hanged by the neck until dead, then drawn and quartered. When the world cries out in protest, Queen Victoria commutes their sentences to banishment for life into the wilderness of Australia.

In 1874, Queen Victoria is astounded to learn that the newly elected Prime Minister of Australia is the same Charles Duffy she banished there twenty-five years ago. Upon the Queen's order, the other eight men are located, and here is what she learns: John Mitchell has become a prominent American politician and his son is now the mayor of New York. Morris Lyene has become the attorney general of Australia, and upon completion of his term, Michael Ireland succeeds him. Thomas McGee is a member of parliament in Canada. Pat Donahue and Terrence McManus are both brigadier generals in the United States Army. Richard O'Gorman is governor general of Newfoundland. Thomas

Meagher, the spokesman who had infuriated the judge, is now the governor of Montana.

Is it merely a coincidence that all nine of these men have risen to positions of leadership and prominence? Or is this simply what happens to people who have the courage of their convictions? I tend to believe the latter.

Is there anything in your life that causes you to feel the passion of these men? Do you, like them, have the courage of your convictions? Is there anything important enough to cause you to speak to the judge as Thomas Meagher did? I am not endorsing their conspiracy against the government; I am speaking of the value of passion.

If there is nothing you would be willing to die for, you have little for which to live. He who would lose his life will find it. ❧

It is easy to be brave from a safe distance.

— Aesop

92

The Seventh Wonder of the World

 OU'VE HEARD OF THE SEVEN WONDERS of the Ancient World, but you probably can't name them. This is because the Seven Wonders are utterly irrelevant to your life today, and most of them no longer exist.

While each of the individual wonders stood for centuries, it was only during the time of Aristotle and his star pupil Alexander (later to be suffixed "the Great") that all seven were in simultaneous existence. Only the oldest of the wonders, the Great Pyramid at Giza, remains with us today.

Yet far more wonderful than the Seven Wonders of the Ancient World are the seven *original* wonders of the world, and all seven of these remain! As a matter of fact, you and I are wonder number six. The seventh wonder is rest.

I write about rest because I greatly fear the disappearance of this wonder from our generation. Were rest an animal, it would certainly head the endangered species list. Its extinction would come at a terrible price.

The original plan was for every seventh day to be set aside for quiet reflection — thinking, unwinding, pondering — not for frantically trying to get caught up on all the things left undone. "Remember the seventh day, and keep it set apart." Was this advice given for the benefit of the Creator? No, it was for the benefit of humankind. Please don't misunderstand me. I'm not talking about religion; I'm talking about our obvious and indisputable need for mental, emotional, and psychological rest.

I am convinced of the wisdom of the original plan because I have seen the results of its abandonment. It seems that rest is under siege today; work and entertainment have placed a bounty on its head, and we collect this bounty with the fierce determination of addicts. We trade rest for movie tickets, career advancement, Little League games, and traffic jams. As a result, we are frazzled, frantic, short tempered, and dissatisfied. Have we forgotten how to rest? Do we think it no longer essential to our mental and emotional well-being? I believe joy and contentment will continue to elude us until we reclaim the gift of rest.

When rest becomes boredom, we have become addicted to work and have forgotten how to sit and think. ೲ

He that can take rest is greater than he that can take cities.

— Benjamin Franklin

The Seven Wonders of the Ancient World

❖ Great Pyramid of Giza
❖ Hanging Gardens of Babylon
❖ Statue of Zeus at Olympia
❖ Temple of Artemis at Ephesus
❖ Mausoleum at Halicarnassus
❖ Colossus at Rhodes
❖ Lighthouse of Pharos Island

WHEN ALEXANDER THE GREAT first turned his ima
that time few scholars knew the extent to which
Aegean. Not to be outdone or outman
and the next seven years saw a

For many yea

93

Is Overchoice
Keeping You Average?

RILLIANT ACCOMPLISHMENTS are nearly always the result of a consuming passion. Whether in business or the arts or marriage or sport, people with passion have a motivation that can rarely be denied. When watching the performance of a passionate player, we often say, "He plays with a lot of heart." This is because passion is the highest form of human motivation.

More important than mere motivation, however, passion also brings focus and commitment. Passionate people are tenacious and undistracted. They have chosen to do one thing well rather than several things badly.

Let me repeat: "They have chosen." Those who experience the joys of the passionate have chosen to reject all options but one. The price of passion is a willingness to say no. Passion can be purchased with no other coin.

The average American cannot say no. This is why he is average. The temptation that defeats the average American is a thing called overchoice, a deceiver that whispers, "You don't have to choose. You can have it all." Overchoice creates a world of too many options.

The word "no" allows us to focus on a single thing, much like a skilled photographer using a camera. By focusing a camera, you exclude everything that isn't essential to the picture — unless, of course, you are the average photographer, in which case your photos show people as small specks floating in an ocean of extraneous background . . . another illustration of overchoice.

A good photographer will get much closer to his subject, excluding everything from the picture except what matters most. The principle of focus is to exclude by choice that which matters less, so that we may give our undivided attention to that which matters most.

What single thing do you most want in your picture? What will you exclude to capture it? Are you willing to ignore things that are less important? Can you say no to overchoice?

Overchoice is a constant temptation, but passion is a way of life. You can do two things halfheartedly or one thing whole-heartedly. Which do you choose? ❧

The lure of the distant and the difficult is deceptive. The great opportunity is where you are.

— John Burroughs

94

The Air Is Full of Ping-Pong Balls

W E ARE BEAT UP, TIRED, AND EXHAUSTED, but it's not the things we're doing that are wearing us out. It's the burden of all the things we're not doing. It's the knowledge of things undone that causes us to wish for more hours in a day. When watching television, it's all the shows we aren't watching that drive us crazy. We have too many possibilities, too little time. Overchoice strikes again.

Overchoice is not only keeping us average, it's making us tired. We delude ourselves with the hope that we can "find time" or "make time" for all the things we'd like to do, yet time can be neither found nor made. Time will continue to sweep past us at its own pace, oblivious to our existence, just as it has since the days of Adam. We cannot manage time; we can only manage ourselves. We will quit feeling tired only when we've learned to say no to overchoice.

One of my senior associates graphically illustrates over-choice with five or six ping-pong balls. Stepping a few feet away, he asks you to catch each of the balls as he gently tosses them to you. You catch the first ball easily — but when Jim tosses the rest of the balls together, you come up empty-handed. Instinctively trying to catch them all, the average person frantically flails the air and sends ping-pong balls careening around the room. The only person who can catch a ball from the group thrown at once is that rare person who will focus on a single ball and ignore all the others.

Do you want to quit feeling tired and overstressed? Quit channel surfing. Ignore all the shows you've chosen not to watch and all the ping-pong balls you've chosen not to catch. We

Americans have more options than are good for us. It's time we said no to overchoice and quit slapping ping-pong balls about the room. ❧

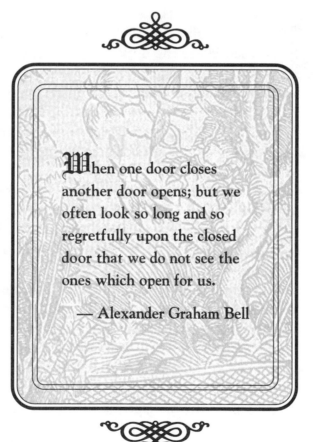

𝔚hen one door closes another door opens; but we often look so long and so regretfully upon the closed door that we do not see the ones which open for us.

— Alexander Graham Bell

95

What Makes Alexander Great?

 LEXANDER IS A DREAMER who inspires everyone around him with visions of grand possibilities. Always the first over the wall of an enemy city, Alex is wounded in the neck at the Granicus River, in the thigh at Issus, and in the shoulder at Gaza, but he never quits fighting, never quits shouting encouragement to his men. A broken leg in Turkestan and a pierced lung in India barely slow him down. Is it any wonder he's never lost a battle?

Alex commits to memory his soldiers' names and deeds, calling each by name when publicly extolling their exploits. He often sends men home to rest and spend time with their families. Is it any wonder they adore him?

In Alexander's presence, common men become radioactive. An unstoppable, natural leader, he conquers all the known world before he is thirty-three and is charging off to conquer the unknown world when he is overtaken by illness and dies.

The life of Alexander profoundly illustrates the difference between leadership and management. Possibly the greatest leader ever to stride the earth, Alexander is a lousy manager. His hatred of bureaucracy and his need for excitement prevent him from building a governmental machine of systems, accountabilities, and procedures. Consequently, his legendary empire disintegrates immediately upon his death.

Not once in the following fifteen hundred years will the Romans have a leader who can fill the shadow of Alexander the Great. Yet their system for management will hold the Roman Empire together decade after decade, century after century, even when grievously incompetent leaders impose amazingly stupid decisions on their people.

Not even the most brilliant manager can do the job of a natural leader, yet even more rarely will a strong leader be a consistent manager. Success is the result of having the right person in the right job at the right time. Are you a leader or a manager? Which does your company need right now? There is a time for revolution and a time for evolution. Which time is this? ❧

STATUE OF LIBERTY, N. Y.

96
Using Your Ruby Red Slippers

OROTHY'S DREAM IS TO GET TO KANSAS, but the people around her are all little Munchkins who have never heard of Kansas and would never consider leaving Munchkinland anyway, so she's off to see the Wizard.

(handwritten, right margin) HAVE YOU EVER BEEN SURROUNDED BY SMALL-MINDED PEOPLE?

Along the way, Dorothy teams up with a Tin Man without a heart and a Scarecrow lacking a brain. Together they enter a dark forest where their greatest fear is that they will be attacked by "lions and tigers and bears, oh my! Lions and tigers and bears." As often happens to the fearful, the first creature they encounter is the one they fear most. (Ironically, the thing we fear most is often the best thing that can happen to us.) The Lion — who, as it happens, claims to be a coward — turns out to be a tremendous ally and becomes an intimate friend.

(handwritten, left margin) YOU KNOW THESE GUYS TOO?

This trio, lacking courage, brains, and heart, must now defeat a wicked witch, flying monkeys, and ugly castle guards. After much hardship and pain, they arrive in Oz, only to realize they already possess the things they sought! The Wizard affirms the bravery of the Lion, the intellect of the Scarecrow, and the heart of the Tin Man with presentations of a medal, a diploma, and a clock.

But what about Dorothy and Kansas?

Struggling, fighting, running, and exasperated, Dorothy has been wearing the ruby red slippers all along. She simply doesn't know how to use them. The secret to accomplishing her dream, says the Wizard, is to concentrate on it with all her might while saying the right words. Voilà! Kansas.

I believe God has given you a dream and your own special pair of ruby red slippers. You have the ability to do great things. Are you concentrating on your goal with all your might? Are you saying the right words? Are you helping the heartless, the frightened, and the foolish around you? Scarecrows, tin men, and cowardly lions are quick to rally 'round a person with a dream. Yes, you need them, but they need you, too.

You are the one with the slippers.

> ℭompared to what we ought to be, we are only half awake. We are making use of only a small part of our physical and mental resources. Stating the thing broadly, the human individual thus lives far within his limits. He possesses power of various sorts which he habitually fails to use.
>
> — William James

97

"But you don't understand."

 ITH THE ADDITION of a single straight line, the following mathematical equation would be correct, and the answer does not involve changing the equals sign:

$$5 + 5 + 5 = 550$$

Before you continue reading, take a moment to see if you can find the solution.

Okay, time's up. Did you solve it? As with most problems, once you've seen the solution, it's painfully obvious. But it requires shifting your perspective.

A new perspective often leads to new answers. Have you ever noticed how easily you can see the answer to a friend's problem? Why is this so? Are you that much smarter than your friend? Or is it because you have the advantage of an outsider's perspective?

And yet — however right you may be — your friend often responds to your advice by saying, "But you don't understand."

What your friend is really saying is "You aren't seeing the problem from my perspective." Thank goodness you're not seeing the problem from his perspective, because from his perspective there is no solution!

Take a few moments to look at your biggest problem from the perspective of an outsider. If someone who didn't understand all the complexities of the situation were examining this problem, what would he suggest? Chances are, that's your answer.

Have you ever seen this definition? Crazy: Doing what you've done before and expecting a different result.

Answers come most easily when we choose to embrace a new perspective. ❧

$$5 + 545 = 550$$

It isn't that they can't see the solution. It is that they can't see the problem.

G. K. Chesterton

98

What Is "Quality of Life"?

'VE ALWAYS BEEN A LITTLE CONFUSED by people who say, "We moved here for the quality of life." Can quality of life be found in a geographic region? "Welcome to Texas, the Quality of Life State," "Come to Connecticut. Our Lives Have More Quality!"

The whole thing reminds me of the days when people would sling a guitar across their backs and hitchhike across the country in a heroic effort to "find themselves." Did you ever notice that not one of these people ever returned to proclaim, "Eureka! I found me! I was hiding out in Texas, the Quality of Life State!"?

I'm sure you'll agree that your quality of life has little to do with where you're living, but would you believe it has just as little to do with what you're doing?

Each of us has known a simple person with a simple job who was happy, and we've also known wealthy people with exciting jobs who would need to cheer up to qualify as miserable.

Quality of life is not a function of where you're living or what you're doing. The quality of your life is determined by who you are being, and you can be whoever you want to be, regardless of where you live or what you do.

Is the person you are being a generous person? Can compassion be found in who you are being? Are you being a true friend? A caring parent? A loving mate? These are the things that will determine the quality of your life. How rare it is to find someone who is genuine, generous, and loving, who is not also deeply contented and profoundly happy!

Forget where you are living and what you are doing. The question to ask yourself is "Who am I being?" ❧

99

Joe Is Not Your Average Boy

OSEPH IS A WEAK AND SICKLY HUNGARIAN teenager with a dream of adventure. Rejected by the Hungarian Army because of his poor eyesight and fragile frame, Joe is accepted by the Union Army of the United States and travels to America to fight in our Civil War.

Miraculously, Joe survives the war and moves to St. Louis, where he accepts a job burying the dead during a cholera epidemic. Three years later, he competes in a special election to fill a seat in the lower house of the state legislature. He wins.

As a legislator, Joe is widely known for fighting corruption in city government. A lobbyist who disagrees with Joe publicly calls him a "damned liar." Joe shoots him. Wounded and outraged, the man tackles Joe and wrestles him to the ground. Joe receives a large gash in his forehead from being pistol whipped with his own gun.

Joe decides the best way to fight is with words and starts a newspaper. His values, techniques, and reckless style of presentation are completely insane in the eyes of the established

press, but newspapers will never be the same. In later years, Joe says, "The trouble with this business is nobody gets drunk anymore."

Immediately upon his return from an extended vacation, Joe is sued by the White House. A furious Theodore Roosevelt demands the retraction of a story. All of America is waiting to see what Joe will do. Trying hard not to show his fear, Joe calmly says, "Mr. Roosevelt is an episode. The [press] is an institution."

America the Beautiful. Where else could a weak and sickly teenager take on the king of the land and win?

A financial magazine recently reported Joe's family to be worth more than one billion dollars, and the prizes given in his name continue to be among the most coveted literary achievements in the world. ❦

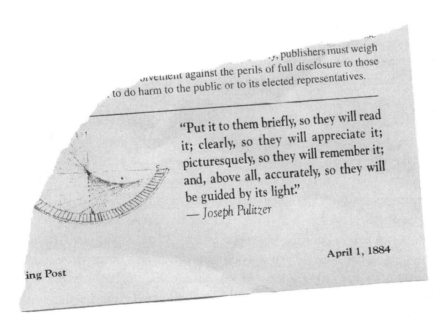

..., publishers must weigh
...vement against the perils of full disclosure to those
... to do harm to the public or to its elected representatives.

"Put it to them briefly, so they will read it; clearly, so they will appreciate it; picturesquely, so they will remember it; and, above all, accurately, so they will be guided by its light."
— Joseph Pulitzer

April 1, 1884

ing Post

100
121,000 Poor People

MERICA DID NOT BECOME what it started out to be, and I, for one, am glad. When Thomas Jefferson penned the Constitution in 1787, only white, male landowners were given the right to vote. Poor men, Africans, Asians, Indians, and women were not entirely "citizens." America was decidedly not the land of opportunity — unless you were wealthy, white, and male.

The structure of society in the New World was very much as it had been in the Old World until 1886, when the Statue of Liberty arrived as a gift from the French. In all America, there was no one among the privileged of 1886 who was willing to undertake the raising of a paltry $100,000 to assemble the Statue of Liberty.

Today's America was born in 1886. The Statue of Liberty would have remained in crates to this very day had it not been for the efforts of an immigrant from Hungary. In his little paper, the *New York World*, Joe Pulitzer appealed to the little people of the city to undertake the installation of the statue. Shoeshine boys, chimney sweeps, machine operators, and grocery clerks were called upon to come to the rescue. In recognition of their heroism, Pulitzer published the name of every contributor, even little kids who gave a nickel.

One of the contributors was a young Jewish woman named Emma Lazarus, who wrote a poem for an art exhibition to help raise money for the statue's installation. Emma's poem closed with the following lines: "Give me your tired, your poor, your huddled masses yearning to breathe free, the wretched refuse of your teeming shore. Send these, the homeless, tempest-tost to me, I lift my lamp beside the golden door!" (I'll bet you thought the government wrote that, didn't you?)

In the end, 121,000 people contributed an average of 83 cents each to erect what has become the most American of all symbols. As a result of his efforts to erect the monument, the circulation of Joe's little paper grew to monumental proportions as well, and Joseph Pulitzer went on to impact our nation as few men have ever done.

America is truly the land of opportunity, where you can become whoever you want. Who is it you want to be? ❧

We must dream of an aristocracy of achievement arising out of a democracy of opportunity.

— Thomas Jefferson

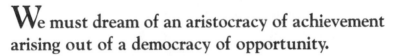

100 + 1
A Message to Garcia

S A YOUNG BOY AT AN AUCTION, I blindly purchased a "box and contents" for seven dollars. In it I found a little pamphlet, published by one Elbert Hubbard in 1899, entitled "A Message to Garcia." I did a little research and discovered that on December 1, 1913, a little more than fourteen years after Elbert Hubbard first wrote his "Message," he penned the following memo:

> Over forty million copies of "A Message to Garcia" have now been printed. This is said to be a larger circulation than any other literary venture has ever attained during the lifetime of the author, in all history — thanks to a series of lucky accidents!

Elbert Hubbard called "A Message to Garcia" a "literary trifle, written one evening after supper in a single hour. It was on the twenty-second of February, eighteen hundred ninety-nine, Washington's birthday, and we were just going to press with the March *Philistine*. The thing leaped hot from my heart, written after a trying day, when I had been endeavoring to train some rather delinquent villagers to abandon the comatose state and get radioactive."

Hubbard went on to say that the article was inspired by an argument with his son, Bert, who suggested that "an obscure lieutenant named Rowan was the real hero of the Cuban War" (today known as the Spanish-American War, in which Teddy Roosevelt led his Rough Riders up San Juan Hill). Bert's argument was that Rowan had "gone alone and done the thing — carried the message to Garcia.

"I then got up from the table and wrote 'A Message to Garcia.' I thought so little of it that we ran it in the [newspaper, as a filler] without a heading. The edition went out, and soon orders began to come for extra copies. A dozen, fifty, a hundred, and when the American News Company ordered a thousand, I asked one of my helpers which article it was that had stirred up the cosmic dust.

"'It's the stuff about Garcia,' he said.

"The next day a telegram came from George H. Daniels, of the New York Central Railroad: 'Give price on one hundred thousand Rowan article in pamphlet form — Empire State Express advertisement on back — also how soon can ship?'

"I replied giving price, and stated we could supply the pamphlets in two years. Our facilities were small and a hundred thousand booklets looked like an awful undertaking."

Hubbard then gave Mr. Daniels permission to reprint the article in his own way, which turned out to be multiple editions of 500,000 copies each. In addition, the article was reprinted in over two hundred magazines and newspapers, and within fourteen years had been translated into scores of other languages.

A Message to Garcia

Elbert Hubbard, 1899

In all this Cuban business there is one man stands out on the horizon of my memory like Mars at perihelion. When war broke out between Spain and the United States, it was very necessary to communicate quickly with the leader of the Insurgents. Garcia was somewhere in the mountain fastnesses of Cuba — no one knew where. No mail or telegraph could reach him. The President must secure his co-operation, and quickly.

What to do!

Someone said to the President, "There's a fellow by the name of Rowan will find Garcia for you, if anybody can."

Rowan was sent for and given a letter to be delivered to Garcia. How "the fellow by name of Rowan" took the letter, sealed it up in an oil-skin pouch, strapped it over his heart, in four days landed by night off the coast of Cuba from an open boat, disappeared into the jungle, and in three weeks came out on the other side of the island, having traversed a hostile country on foot, and having delivered his letter to Garcia, are things I have no special desire now to tell in detail.

The point I wish to make is this: McKinley gave Rowan a letter to be delivered to Garcia; Rowan took the letter and did not ask, "Where is he at?" By the Eternal! There is a man whose form should be cast in deathless bronze and the statue placed in every college in the land. It is not book-learning young men need, nor instruction about this or that, but a stiffening of the vertebrae which will cause them to be loyal to a trust, to act promptly, concentrate their energies; do the thing — "carry a message to Garcia!"

General Garcia is dead now, but there are other Garcias.

No man, who has endeavored to carry out an enterprise where many hands were needed, but has been well-nigh appalled at times by the imbecility of the average man — the inability or unwillingness to concentrate on a thing and do it. Slipshod assistance, foolish inattention, dowdy indifference, and half-hearted work seem the rule; and no man succeeds, unless by hook or crook, or threat, he forces or bribes other men to assist him; or mayhap, God in His goodness performs a miracle, and sends him an Angel of Light for an assistant. You, reader, put this matter to a test: You are sitting now in your office — six clerks are within your call. Summon any one and make this request: "Please look in the encyclopedia and make a brief memorandum for me concerning the life of Corregio."

Will the clerk quietly say, "Yes, sir," and go do the task?

On your life, he will not. He will look at you out of a fishy eye, and ask one or more of the following questions:

Who was he?

Which encyclopedia?

Where is the encyclopedia?

Was I hired for that?

Don't you mean Bismarck?

What's the matter with Charlie doing it?

Is he dead?

Is there any hurry?

Shan't I bring you the book and let you look it up yourself?

What do you want to know for?

And I will lay you ten to one that after you have answered the questions, and explained how to find the information, and why you want it, the clerk will go off and get one of the other clerks to help him find Garcia — and then come back and tell you there is no such man. Of course I may lose my bet, but according to the Law of Average, I will not.

Now if you are wise you will not bother to explain to your "assistant" that Corregio is indexed under the C's, not in the K's, but you will smile sweetly and say, "Never mind," and go look it up yourself.

And this incapacity for independent action, this moral stupidity, this infirmity of the will, this unwillingness to cheerfully catch hold and lift, are the things that put pure socialism so far into the future. If men will not act for themselves, what will they do when the benefit of their effort is for all? A first mate with knotted club seems necessary; and the dread of getting "the bounce" Saturday night holds many a worker in his place.

Advertise for a stenographer, and nine times out of ten who apply can neither spell nor punctuate — and do not think it necessary to.

Can such a one write a letter to Garcia?

"You see that bookkeeper," said the foreman to me in a large factory.

"Yes, what about him?"

"Well, he's a fine accountant, but if I'd send him to town on an errand, he might accomplish the errand all right, and, on the other hand, might stop at four saloons on the way, and when he got to Main Street, would forget what he had been sent for."

Can such a man be entrusted to carry a message to Garcia?

We have recently been hearing much maudlin sympathy expressed for the "down-trodden denizen of the sweat shop" and the "homeless wanderer searching for honest employment," and with it all often go many hard words for the men in power.

Nothing is said about the employer who grows old before his time in a vain attempt to get frowsy ne'er-do-wells to do intelligent work; and his long patient striving with "help" that does nothing but loaf when his back is turned. In every store and factory there is a constant weeding-out process going on. The employer is constantly sending away "help" that have shown their incapacity to further the interests of the business, and others are being taken on. No matter how good times are, this sorting continues, only if times are hard and work is scarce, this sorting is done finer — but out and forever out, the incompetent and unworthy go. It is the survival of the fittest. Self-interest prompts every employer to keep the best — those who can carry a message to Garcia.

I know one man of really brilliant parts who has not the ability to manage a business of his own, and yet who is absolutely worthless to anyone else, because he carries with him constantly the insane suspicion that his employer is oppressing, or intending to oppress, him. He can not give orders, and he will not receive them. Should a message be given him to take to Garcia, his answer would probably be, "Take it yourself."

Tonight this man walks the streets looking for work, the wind whistling through his threadbare coat. No one who knows him dare employ him, for he is a regular firebrand of discontent. He is impervious to reason, and the only thing that can impress him is the toe of a thick-soled No. 9 boot.

Of course I know that one so morally deformed is no less to be pitied than a physical cripple; but in your pitying, let us drop a tear, too, for the men who are striving to carry on a great enterprise, whose working hours are not limited by the whistle, and whose hair is fast turning white through the struggle to hold the line in dowdy indifference, slipshod imbecility, and the heartless ingratitude which, but for their enterprise, would be both hungry and homeless.

Have I put the matter too strongly? Possibly I have; but when all the world has gone a-slumming I wish to speak a word of sympathy for the man who succeeds — the man who, against great odds, has directed the efforts of others, and, having succeeded, finds there's nothing in it: nothing but bare board and clothes.

I have carried a dinner-pail and worked for a day's wages, and I have also been an employer of labor, and I know there is something to be said on both sides. There is no excellence, per se, in poverty; rags are no recommendation; and all employers are not rapacious and high-handed, any more than all poor men are virtuous.

My heart goes out to the man who does his work when the "boss" is away, as well as when he is home. And the man who, when given a letter for Garcia, quietly takes the missive, without asking any idiotic questions, and with no lurking intention of chucking it into the nearest sewer, or of doing aught else but deliver it, never gets "laid off," nor has to go on strike for higher wages. Civilization is one long anxious search for just such individuals. Anything such a man asks will be granted; his kind is so rare that no employer can afford to let him go. He is wanted in every city, town, and village — in every office, shop, store and factory. The world cries out for such; he is needed, and needed badly — the man who can carry a message to Garcia. ❧

Index

About the Author

A CONTEMPLATIVE OBSERVER, Roy H. Williams has been a lifelong student of the human race, forever seeking to answer the question, "What makes people do the things they do?"

Roy indulges his fascination with the future and the past by reading science fiction and historical biographies. He writes poetry, advertising, and screenplays. He's a riveting public speaker, but hates to travel: "On the third morning away from Pennie, I wake up with a cold sore on my lip. Maybe when the boys are older, she can travel with me and I won't be so miserable."

A collector of antiques and old books, pocket watches, fountain pens, vintage photographs, and automotive memorabilia, Roy is a self-described "pack rat." (Pennie agrees.) They have two sons, Rex and Jake.

Roy H. Williams Marketing, Inc., headquartered near Austin, Texas, creates controversial ad campaigns for small business clients in thirty-eight states. The firm occasionally hosts advertising seminars that are attended by business owners and students from around the world. ❧

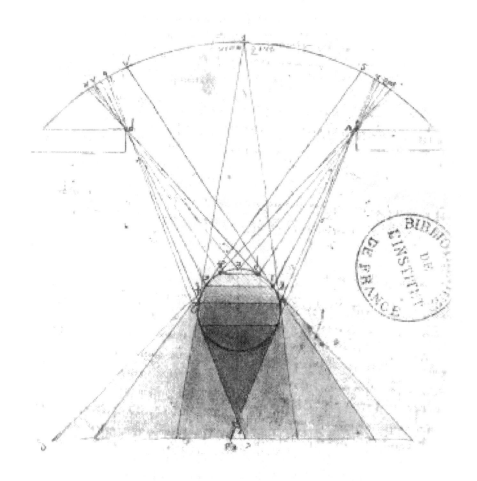

For additional copies of

The Wizard of Ads

Turning Words into Magic
and Dreamers into Millionaires

$16.95 paperback
$26.95 hardcover

visit your favorite bookstore

or call toll-free
1-800-945-3132
or fax your order to 512-288-5055.

Visa / MasterCard / Discover / American Express are accepted.

Quantity discounts are available.

On audio:

The Wizard of Ads

An unabridged book
read by the Wizard himself

5 hours on 8 cassettes
$39.95 + $3.95 shipping & handling
available only from 1-800-218-2736

BARD PRESS

512-329-8373 voice
512-329-6051 fax
www.bardpress.com